"Keats called it Negative Capability—the skill 'of being in uncertainties, Mysteries, doubts.' Tom Thibodeau, coach of the Chicago Bulls, says, 'You gotta learn to be comfortable being uncomfortable.' But nobody has nailed this faculty like Jonathan Fields, showing us how to turn the fog of self-doubt, fear, and internal paralysis into the clear sailing of focus, concentration, and results."

—Steven Pressfield, author of *The War of Art* and *Do the Work*

"Jonathan Fields's new book is brilliant and subversive. Through sharp insights and practical exercises, he reframes doubt, hesitation, and ambiguity as gateways to our own natural brilliance. It's a handbook for fearless creativity and its offshoots: meaning, authenticity, and true success."

—Susan Piver, author of *The Wisdom of a Broken Heart* and *How Not to Be Afraid of Your Own Life*

"Fields is a breezy, engaging writer who demystifies creativity with a whole new bag of user-friendly tricks and practices—crux moves, circuit breakers, certainty anchors, and attentional training. Hugely practical. Lean into *Uncertainty*"

—Tony Schwartz, author of *Be Excellent at Anything*

e chasm between idea and action is bridged by clarity. *Uncer-* clarifies the steps and helps you get to the other side."

—Julien Smith, coauthor of *Trust Agents*

ainty matters. If you wait until the fear is gone, you will never you will rarely do anything that matters."

—Seth Godin, author of *Linchpin* and *Purple Cow*

ertain. Embracing that paralyzes most people, but it also all number of brave individuals driven to create extraor- usinesses, and lives. This b minds of the world's greatest creators. It's an essential tool to transform uncertainty and fear into power and genius."

—Kris Carr, author of *Crazy Sexy Diet* and
Crazy Sexy Cancer Tips

"*Uncertainty* is a great gift, a marvelous book. Jonathan calls out the elephant in our lives, the fear of failure, and gives us the insights, the rituals, and the presence of mind to tame it. Unless your life is limited to death and taxes, uncertainty is omnipresent. This book empowers the reader to gratefully accept the risks of a life worth living.

—Randy Komisar, author of *The Monk and the Riddle*

"Groundbreaking. Highly practical. Über provoking. This special and rare book will help you change the game in a world of deep uncertainty."

—Robin Sharma, author of *The Leader Without a Title*

"A huge key to success is understanding the real mental blocks that can stop an otherwise great new project in its tracks. Another is knowing how to overcome them. Fields provides powerful tools for getting from the glimmer of an idea to a successful outcome and managing all the hard stuff that happens in-between."

—Bob Burg, author of *The Go Giver*

"The only thing certain in business is that nothing is certain. Fields's unique combination of practical and creative skills and solutions help transform uncertainty from a source of fear into fuel for action."

—Carol Roth, author of *The Entrepreneur Equatic*

"The most successful people in the world are comfortable with d comfort, embrace uncertainty, and have fun with fear. Read this b liant book and you will too."

—Michael Port, author of *The Think Big Mani*

"If you're up to anything big, then what you're attempting has p bly never been done before. Which means you're face-to-face with that great, terrifying void called uncertainty. We all need help to get through that void; Jonathan's book is an invaluable guide to carry you safely to success in the face of fear."

—Michael Ellsberg, author of *The Education of Millionaires*

"People hate uncertainty—not just on a gut level but at a deep neurological level. But there's a proven correlation between comfort with ambiguity and creativity. And we live in an age where creativity is an inherent part of personal and organizational success. So what to do? The answer's here—insights, stories, and practices—in Jonathan Fields's wise and practical book."

—Michael Bungay Stainer, author of *Do More Great Work*

"Jonathan Fields has taken the broadest of horizons—the role of uncertainty in the creative act—and distilled it into a highly readable, immediately actionable tool kit of insights, techniques, and practices that I guarantee will revolutionize how—and why—you do what you do. If you do any sort of work that involves the act of creation (and these days, who doesn't?), you must read this book."

—Les McKeown, author of *Predictable Success*

"Fear keeps scores of people stuck in careers and lives they hate. Fields gives crystal clear guidance on how to engage with uncertainty so that it fuels creativity and action. Your productivity, happiness, and pocketbook will be massively improved by reading this book."

—Pamela Slim, author of *Escape from Cubicle Nation*

PORTFOLIO / PENGUIN

UNCERTAINTY

Jonathan Fields is a NYC dad, husband, serial entrepreneur, award-winning author, blogger, and business strategist. His last book, *Career Renegade,* was named a Top 10 Small Biz Book by *Small Business Trends,* and *Uncertainty* was named the #1 Personal Development Book of 2011 by 800-CEO-READ. Fields writes about entrepreneurship, innovation, and lifestyles at JonathanFields.com; runs his lifestyle/biz-training venture, GoodLifeProject.com; speaks around the world; and is regularly featured in the media.

UNCERTAINTY

Turning Fear and Doubt into Fuel for **Brilliance**

Jonathan Fields

PORTFOLIO | PENGUIN

PORTFOLIO / PENGUIN
Published by the Penguin Group
Penguin Group (USA) Inc., 375 Hudson Street, New York, New York 10014, USA
Penguin Group (Canada), 90 Eglinton Avenue East, Suite 700, Toronto, Ontario M4P 2Y3, Canada (a division of
Pearson Penguin Canada Inc.)
Penguin Books Ltd, 80 Strand, London WC2R 0RL, England
Penguin Ireland, 25 St Stephen's Green, Dublin 2, Ireland (a division of Penguin Books Ltd)
Penguin Group (Australia), 707 Collins Street, Melbourne, Victoria 3008, Australia
(a division of Pearson Australia Group Pty Ltd)
Penguin Books India Pvt Ltd, 11 Community Centre, Panchsheel Park, New Delhi–110 017, India
Penguin Group (NZ), 67 Apollo Drive, Rosedale, Auckland 0632, New Zealand (a division of Pearson
New Zealand Ltd)
Penguin Books, Rosebank Office Park, 181 Jan Smuts Avenue, Parktown North 2193, South Africa
Penguin China, B7 Jaiming Center, 27 East Third Ring Road North, Chaoyang District, Beijing 100020, China

Penguin Books Ltd, Registered Offices:
80 Strand, London WC2R 0RL, England

First published in the United States of America by Portfolio / Penguin, a member of
Penguin Group (USA) Inc. 2011
This paperback edition published 2012

10 9 8 7 6 5 4 3 2 1

THE LIBRARY OF CONGRESS HAS CATALOGED THE HARDCOVER EDITION AS FOLLOWS:
Fields, Jonathan.
Uncertainty : turning fear and doubt into fuel for brilliance / Jonathan Fields.
p.   cm.
Includes index.
ISBN 978-1-59184-424-2 (hc.)
ISBN 978-1-59184-566-9 (pbk.)
1. Risk taking (Psychology)   2. Uncertainty.   3. Creative ability.   4. Creative ability in business.   5.
Entrepreneurship—Psychological aspects.   6. Success.   7. Success in business.   I. Title.
BF637.R57F54 2011
650.1—dc23
2011019058

Printed in the United States of America
Set in Fairfield LT Std • Designed by Victoria Hartman

To Jesse and Stephanie:
You make it all possible.

CONTENTS

INTRODUCTION

THE SHAPE-SHIFTER

RANDY KOMISAR IS a bit of a legend in Silicon Valley. He started his career as a lawyer, then moved over to the business side of things, running LucasArts Entertainment and serving as CEO of Crystal Dynamics in the '90s. He was gearing up to become CEO of a bigger, perhaps public company. A fairly linear path lay before him, and he was executing on it masterfully. But Komisar began to notice something he didn't expect. He was becoming more and more successful on a path that was making him less and less happy.

So, in his words, he "jumped out of a perfectly fine airplane at Crystal Dynamics and just took off in midair." He abandoned the safe path for a guy with his brains, abilities, and track record and decided to wing it, to create his career and his life from that moment forward by leaning into what made him come alive. There was no longer a blueprint for how he was going to spend the next ten or fifteen years of his life.

While others might have experienced that awareness as paralyzing, Komisar viewed it as immensely freeing. Energizing. It enabled him to think about his life and career from that moment forward very differently. The constraints of success no longer inhibited his ability to create what came next, so he started to reinvent himself. He began to see opportunities he never would have been open to before.

Komisar was looking for a way to interact with great entrepreneurs across a variety of ideas in a meaningful role. He didn't know what that was. He didn't know how to get paid. He didn't know if it would be the same role in every company. He didn't know what he'd do or not do. All he knew was he was going to put one foot down in front of the other in that direction. There was no map. No proof of concept. No promises of success.

Randy Komisar literally created a new job category, the Virtual CEO, around what he saw as a peculiar set of qualities and experiences he had and the specific needs of Silicon Valley during the start-up boom of the late '90s. At that time, there were insufficient resources to lead organizations, and the entrepreneurs coming up were not experienced entrepreneurs. They needed what Komisar had to offer.

In the role of Virtual CEO for legendary tech companies like WebTV and TiVo, Komisar partnered with entrepreneurs to help them grow themselves and their ideas into great businesses. As he put it, "I served as consigliere without displacing them, rolling up my sleeves to work through all the bits of building their businesses— strategy, recruiting, partnering, financing, leadership—the whole gamut. Their individual development was as important to me as the development of the business." Some things didn't work, some things did work, and the idea got a lot of attention and ultimately served as a model for people who would eventually follow in his footsteps.

Komisar's exposure as a Virtual CEO then opened up another entirely unforeseen opportunity. Harvard Business School Press was looking to publish some interesting new books during the boom. The editor at the time, Hollis Heimbouch, flew out to the Valley and invited Komisar for coffee at the Konditorei, the coffee shop that served as his unofficial office. She said, "Let's begin just writing a book." Komisar's first answer was no, because he felt he had nothing to say.

By the next morning, he had changed his tune. He said, "If you're willing to give me a shot to do something completely different, I'm going to write a book that's a business book but not a business book. It's not going to be your typical Harvard business book. It's not going to have thirteen chapters to tell you how to do something. It's going to be full of ambiguity, uncertainty. It's going to lay out the bread crumbs, but it's not going to lay out the path."

Heimbouch said yes. With that, the fable-driven classic and national bestseller *The Monk and the Riddle* (2000) was born. Out of the book came a teaching position at Stanford University that eventually led to Komisar's current incarnation as a partner in the legendary Sand Hill Road venture capital firm Kleiner Perkins Caufield & Byers.

THE CHANGE MAKER

Marie Forleo is a force of nature. A former fitness and dance instructor who traveled and presented around the world as part of the Nike team, she knows how to command a stage. Forleo doesn't know the meaning of the word "no." She self-published her first book, selling 8,000 copies on her own before it was picked up by a publisher (it's now available in nine languages). A few years back, Forleo began to realize she'd built not only a strong personal brand but a real business. And she'd become fascinated by the idea of creating a completely location-independent company. She began to devour information on entrepreneurship and marketing, learning from some of the world's top marketers and entrepreneurs, then turning around and sharing what she was learning with a market she deeply connected with—women entrepreneurs.

She started with lower-priced trainings, coaching, and information products and was growing a nice business, consistently pushing her comfort zone as she grew. But it was her decision to make a huge leap in her brand in 2009 that left her shaking with anxiety. She'd discovered the concept of mastermind groups. These were generally groups of like-minded entrepreneurs or professionals who would pay to gather in the presence of a group organizer, usually a high-profile achiever in the field, and discuss business. Lower-priced mastermind groups would get together by phone, but the higher-priced ones would convene in person at a hotel or some other location.

Forleo was fascinated by this model in part because of how much potential it had to have a direct, ongoing impact on careers, aspirations, and lives, but also because of how much higher the price point was than the services she'd been offering. Moving her business to the level of offering mastermind groups and charging fifteen times the price of her existing highest-ticket service would mean a giant leap in income, reach, and fun.

The problem was that she had issues with the way mastermind groups were traditionally run. They were formulaic, stodgy, held in conference rooms, and often focused entirely on business, without reference to how the participants' lives interacted with their companies. Forleo wanted to create an experience that was radically different on every level. Something that would redefine masterminding. Something that had never been done before. That elated her . . . and terrified her. But more inspired than paralyzed, she set to work.

Forleo's experience would be built around exotic locations and adventures that wouldn't be revealed until the last minute. While they wouldn't exclude men, they'd largely be tailored toward the lives and fantasies of women entrepreneurs. They would incorporate not only extensive business and marketing training, but a wide range of lifestyle-driven conversations and activities that ranged from making a music video to pole dancing to using business to drive social change. They would be about enduring relationships and spiritual transformation. And they would cost serious money—$15,000 (which at last glance had bumped up to $20,000) a year—with only as-needed access to her between quarterly excursions.

Pulling off this idea would mean a massive leap forward for her business and her reputation as an entrepreneur, thought leader, and marketer. If she crashed and burned, especially in what would be a public way, it could be devastating. It's hard to sell mastery of entrepreneurship, marketing, and lifestyle without being able to succeed at those very things in your own business and life. This was Forleo's moment to face the unknown, to lean into uncertainty, risk her reputation, and expose herself to judgment—all in the name of creating, building, and serving on a new level. Anxious, shaking, concerned but hopeful, she went public with her vision with a video made on her Flip camera.

The response was instant. People said yes. They'd never seen or heard of anything like what Forleo was planning to deliver. They wanted in. With that, the Rich, Happy & Hot Adventure Mastermind was born. Forleo's continued willingness to embrace uncertainty and fear, rather than run from them, has allowed her to now expand the brand to include an annual conference in New York, offshoot online programs, and tremendous business growth. Because it's close to her heart, it's given her the ability to give a lot more back.

In 2010, only a year after "the big leap," Forleo had grown her business to the point where she was able to launch an initiative called Change Your Life, Change the World, through which she gave 5% of the net profits of her online coaching program to women-focused philanthropy. This led to a partnership with Richard Branson's Virgin Unite Foundation. In early 2011, Forleo accompanied Branson and a small group of entrepreneurs interested in using business for social change on a "connection trip" to Africa, where they visited selected Virgin Unite–funded initiatives, including various clinics, the Branson Centre of Entrepreneurship, orphanages, and schools. It was one of the most extraordinary experiences of her life and, for her, a signpost of much bigger work to come.

THE FILMMAKER

For fifteen years leading up to October 15, 2008, Erik Proulx was a copywriter at a number of large advertising agencies. A week earlier, he'd been told a promotion to Associate Creative Director was on its way, along with a nice raise. That was great news. Proulx enjoyed what he did; he was a married father of two with a house in a suburb of Boston, so the extra money would come in handy. Maybe even, for the first time, he'd be able to start putting some money away for the future.

When he got the call on the 15th, though, he wasn't sure what to expect. Since he'd been told he was about to be promoted, people all around him were being laid off. Sure enough, instead of getting a promotion, he was asked to leave. To this day, he remembers the only two words his career-executioner said: "Sorry, dude."

Proulx was angry, sad, frustrated, and concerned about the future of his family. His modest savings wouldn't cover them for long. And while he was thankful when new offers came in for copywriting jobs that were pretty similar to the position he'd just lost, for some reason, as each offer arrived, he kept saying no. Something in him had changed. A fire had been lit, but he wasn't quite sure what was burning—or where it would lead him. While he loved the creative part of advertising, especially the storytelling aspect, he didn't enjoy working on campaigns for clients and products he could care less about. He didn't like the lack of security of being only as good as your last campaign. And he didn't want to go back.

So with a family to support, a house, a mortgage, and no income, he did the only logical thing: He became a documentary filmmaker.

Proulx had become possessed by the desire to tell the stories of the thousands who were being fired in his industry (remember, this was October 2008, the beginning of mass economic destruction) but had somehow reframed their demise as permission to finally do what they were here on Earth to do. He'd never made a film before. He had no money to do it, let alone pay his monthly living expenses. But there was no question about this movie's being made. This was his moment, and the movie *Lemonade* (2009) was the thing Proulx couldn't not do.

Was he afraid? Absolutely. Terrified? Maybe. Uncertain of nearly everything beyond the fact that this was what he wanted to do? Yes. Still, Proulx posted his intention on his blog. He tweeted it out and posted it on Facebook. Hours later, the advertising industry news mammoth *Ad Age* picked up the story. *Holy crap*, Proulx thought. There would be no turning back now—he had gone public. Whether he succeeded or failed, *Lemonade* was his to own.

From this public commitment, it seems, as W. H. Murray recounted in *The Scottish Himalayan Expedition* (1951), "all manner of unforeseen incidents, meetings and material assistance, which no man could have dreamt" came his way. His passion, his energy, his willingness to do whatever it took to tell a story that so many wanted to hear, at a time of great despair, propelled the quest. He needed cameras to film, but had no money. Sony made them appear. He needed to get to Los Angeles to interview four people but couldn't afford the airfare. He tweeted and posted his dilemma online. Two hours later VirginAmerica stepped up to cover his travel. Film and sound people and color correctors rallied to the cause. Top movie editors and production houses donated time to help turn hours and hours of footage into thirty-six minutes of genius.

I remember sitting on a large slab of granite with Proulx on the southern edge of Manhattan's Central Park shortly after the movie came out. He was scrambling to piece together contract work while traveling around, showing the movie in small venues, and hustling to get distribution deals. It was a time filled with triumph but also with a new wave of self-doubt. The movie was done. It had been very well received but had been rejected by the major festivals that would have opened the way to major distribution money. The quest had crested.

Proulx wanted to keep telling stories that meant something. But he'd already put his family through so much. They were leveraged to the hilt, and though his wife was still his greatest champion, he was fairly certain they'd have to give up the house in which he wanted desperately to be able to live out his days. Scale down and move to another state where they knew nobody but could live more affordably.

I asked Proulx why he thought he had to make a choice between a job and being a filmmaker who tells stories that touched people. Why couldn't he do both? The world had rallied to support him once. There was no reason he couldn't keep making movies, using the same hustle that made the first movie happen to now line up enough advertising gigs to support his family and keep paying his mortgage. It might take a little longer to make a film. But so what?

And that's exactly what he did. A new quest was born. Four days before turning in this manuscript, I spent an hour catching up with Proulx. The night before, he'd paid off a $16,000 credit card bill. He was still in debt, but an albatross had been lifted: he was making good money with his unconventional blended career. And he was well into his next film, *Lemonade: Detroit* (2011).

• • •

In rock climbing, each route from the ground to the peak is rated with a number. A climb rated 4.0 or lower is considered nontechnical. You need strength and agility, but not equipment. A climb rated 5.0 and higher requires ropes, harnesses, other protective gear, and a bit more experience. Climbing at a godlike 5.14 level requires years of training, practice, less than 5% body fat, and a will of steel.

The interesting thing about these ratings is that they aren't based so much on the difficulty of the entire climb as on a set of moves known as the crux. Crux moves are the most challenging moments of the entire route; they often require you to push physically, emotionally, and intellectually, to take big and often blind risks in a way no other part of the climb does. There may be multiple crux moves along a single route. The manner in which you handle the thousands of smaller moments of uncertainty and challenge along the way determines whether you get to the crux moves. But the way you handle the crux moves themselves so strongly determines whether you'll actually reach the peak that the difficulty of the most challenging crux sequence is often used to rate the entire climb.

Any worthwhile creative endeavor has its own crux moves. Your project may be defined in part by your day-to-day decisions and actions, but what really determines whether you succeed or fail—whether you're starting a business, developing a new product, making a film, or writing a book—is how you respond during a series of pivotal moments—the creation crux moves.

These are the moments the creators on the previous pages faced and will continue to face as their journeys evolve. Marie Forleo met hers when she decided to stake her business and career on a big risk and bring her secret vision to a completely untested public. Randy Komisar's unfolded the moment he chose to, in his words, "jump out of a perfectly fine airplane," and when each subsequent leap into something new introduced more challenge. Erik Proulx's first big one was the decision to reject a return to the career that was paying his bills but emptying his soul and instead to live and die in a very public way by doing what nobody else would dare to do.

These creation crux moves are the moments when the legends and stories of every great artist, entrepreneur, corporate innovator, and quest-driven visionary are born. They are punctuated by the opportunity to rise above what Theodore Roosevelt called the "gray twilight that knows neither victory nor defeat" and lay claim to genius.

This is where the magic happens . . . if it doesn't kill you along the way.

THE THREE PSYCHIC HORSEMEN OF CREATION

One of the single greatest determinants of high-level success as an innovator or creator in any realm is the ability to manage and at times even seek out sustained high levels of uncertainty, bundled lovingly with risk of loss and exposure to criticism.

These three psychic horsemen of creation must often not only be sought, but embraced repeatedly and with increasing levels of intensity over extended periods of time. In fact, they are often signposts that you've entered your next big creation crux move. In the context of a single endeavor, you may need to live in this place for hours, days, months, or years until the project takes on enough form to prove the validity of the vision. In the context of the desire to build an extraordinary career, legacy, business, or body of work, we're talking a lifetime of returning to that place again and again. For those driven to create something extraordinary from nothing, there is no end. There are only ebbs and flows.

The problem is, the vast majority of creators across all fields, from painters to entrepreneurs and writers to CEOs, are horribly equipped to handle the fear, angst, and anxiety that ride along with these critical moments. And it's this very failure, much more so than a lack of creativity or vision, that destroys so many endeavors and careers—and at times even the creators themselves.

Oddly, nobody talks about this. Most people just assume you either have the magical ability to lean into uncertainty, risk, and exposure or you don't. In a recent keynote address before 500 of the world's top creatives at the 99% Conference in New York City in 2010, Rhode Island School of Design president John Maeda spoke about the critical importance of being able to endure tremendous levels of creative ambiguity. He argued that one of the things that makes creative people different is that they "love mistakes" and are "completely okay with ambiguity."

"It's quite natural," he said.

But is it really? Is your ability to handle the uncertainty, risk, and exposure that are integral to the quest, especially at the critical moments, simply a matter of whether or not you landed in the right gene pool? Are all high-level creators simply natural-born fear alchemists, able to magically transform their fear into a positive force? And if you've been blessed with the compulsion to create, but not the seeming organic ability to live in the question without pain, does that mean your only resort is suffering or self-medication?

Or are there things you and the organizations you work within can do that will allow you not only to endure but embrace the purported dark side as fuel for creation? To invite uncertainty, take risks, and expose yourself to criticism in the quest for brilliant outcomes? Most important, can those things be taught?

DECODING THE CREATION MIND-SET

Uncertainty is about what goes on in your head, your heart, and your gut as you strive to create anything truly extraordinary. It's about the nutty things we do, the gremlins we battle, the decisions we make and actions we take in the pursuit of long-term, large-scale creative, artistic, entrepreneurial, and organizational greatness.

The book begins with an in-depth exploration of the three psychic horsemen of creation: uncertainty, risk, and exposure to criticism. We'll uncover why they lead to so much suffering and why, in spite of the havoc they so often wreak, they must remain present. We'll also look at what happens when you try to snuff them out instead of embracing and even amplifying them.

We will explore the myth of the natural fear alchemist and discover how most of these "freaks of nature" are actually just as terrified as you but have adopted a set of personal practices, workflow adaptations, and have created or found themselves in environments that are built to support innovation and creation and that allow them to lean into the fear and anxiety.

Then we'll dive into those transformational personal practices, workflow and situational changes—the ones that let you feel the uncertainty, risk, and exposure necessary to high-level creation, but experience them more as opportunity rather than deep suffering, anxiety, and paralysis.

The book then will take a bold leap into the world of Creation 2.0, exploring what happens when you turn loose next-generation "social" creative and business processes—like lean methodology, rapid iteration, and community co-creation—on the worlds of entrepreneurship and traditional art. You'll discover how to adapt these approaches to radically enhance the creative output and speed of the process without bastardizing your ethos or diluting your output. You will learn how these approaches, artfully leveraged, can profoundly change the deeper psychology of creation and inject a serious shot of humanity into the journey. You will also learn to build these tools and strategies into the fabric and culture of your endeavor, allowing them to fuel your own creative efforts and the work of those charged with moving the venture forward on all levels.

Finally, we'll look at an age-old question: How do you know when to hold and when to fold? We'll explore how so many people misinterpret the relief from anxiety when you pull away from the creative process as reclaiming peace of mind instead of what it so often is: the fleeting sensation of dreams dying. Then we'll consider a set of questions and metrics that rise above the amorphous answer "You just know," often offered almost by rote, and provide a more rational framework for making what is so often a brutally difficult call.

If you're someone with a natural and unrelenting ability to lean into risk, judgment, and uncertainty on a level that allows you to make what nobody else can make, this book will show you how to do it better, faster, and with less suffering (and, no, suffering is not mandatory).

If you feel organically unable to survive the angst of creation long enough to bring genius to life, we're about to hack the system for you. This book will give you a better understanding of your own creative process and a set of concrete daily practices and environmental changes that will allow you to reframe uncertainty, risk, and exposure as allies for creating and innovating on a level you never thought possible.

1

WHY UNCERTAINTY MATTERS

WHETHER YOU'RE WORKING on a team charged with driving business innovation, writing a novel, choreographing a dance, starting a company, or coding an app, the creative process follows a similar overarching progression. It starts with a question—one that's different for every quest and every creator.

When you begin, nothing is certain save the drive to create something worth the effort. The more certain you are of the answer or the outcome in advance, the more likely it is to have been done already—to be derivative—and the less anyone will care, including you. Anything certain has already been done.

From this place of unknown possibilities and endings, the process moves through its many phases and creation crux moves. Information is gathered, options explored, hooks laid down, colors mixed, numbers crunched, and experiments completed. Countless decisions have been made, new ideas formed, tested, expanded, and killed, until finally the endeavor reaches a place of maximum constraint or final form. An amorphous idea becomes words in a printed book. Feelings about movement, light, color, and energy become oil on canvas. Riffs, beats, hooks, and choruses become completed tracks. Music and movement become a dance. Numbers, processes, forms, and functions become platforms. A desire to serve a community and take away its pain becomes a business, a service, a solution.

The progression, however, is anything but a straight line. In the early days, in order to justify action, risk, investment, and exposure to criticism, you need to make assumptions. Some are based on fact, but others are outright leaps of faith. Along the way, while some will be validated, others will be eviscerated, proven to have been anything from near misses to complete garbage.

In the world of entrepreneurship, one of the happiest days in the life of a start-up founder is the day she gets funded. It puts money in the bank, and it's a huge vote of confidence in the team, the vision, the business, and the model. The smartest investors out there are saying, "Yes, we believe in you." The problem is, more often than not, that smart money, along with the founders themselves, are utterly wrong. The business they've all rallied around is built upon bad information that is soon to be disproven on a level that, without adaptation, will tank the business and vanish the investment.

When these moments along the creation path happen, you have a choice to make. You can strap on your vision blinders, ignore the fact that you've gone off the rails, and keep to your original plan. Or you can stand up and make a conscious choice to wade back into uncertain waters, knowing you've now invested time, money, and energy in an endeavor that, without substantial alteration, is going to end up a dud. These are tough moments, and ones that no creator in any realm can avoid.

The chart on page 17 shows the uncertainty dynamic over time in nearly any creative process.

The big jumps in uncertainty are the creation crux moves. For a painter, it might be the moment you come face to face with the fact

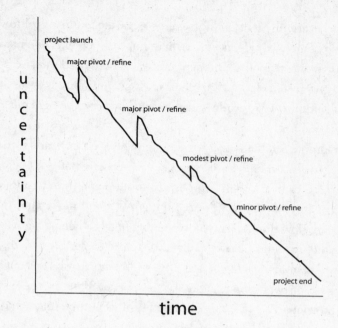

that your current painting or collection just isn't working. For an entrepreneur, it might be when you've gained enough information to prove your assumptions wrong. For a development team leader or hacker, it could be an awakening to the understanding that the solution you've been developing won't do what you want it to. Notice also that in addition to the big realizations and changes in course, the line itself is jagged. This represents the understanding that at no point does uncertainty entirely go away. It's always there, offering up a constant stream of less disruptive questions and challenges.

We'll spend a lot more time focusing on how to recognize these moments and what to do about them. We'll find that these moments often come not only with elevated levels of uncertainty, but with two other psychic horsemen of innovation—exposure to judgment and risk of loss. Just like uncertainty, their existence is mandatory, despite their destructive potential.

For many, even the possibility of being criticized takes you sailing back to every moment of angst you've experienced in your life when you felt somehow judged for not living up to someone else's or even your own expectations. Judgment is often experienced as pain, but it's really just feedback data. All that angst surrounding it is just emotional sludge, the by-product of tactless delivery or the creator's own hang-ups.

Creators need data. They need judgment, feedback, and criticism. Without them, there's no way to know whether what you're creating is working or not. When you base your actions on random guesses, rather than on relevant information, growth and movement toward brilliance slow dramatically or grind to a halt. Kill constructive judgment and you retard growth, adaptation, and evolution.

The same applies to the risk of loss. Whenever you set out to do what's never been done before, or never been done in the way you want to do it, you risk losing all sorts of things—time that could have been spent doing something else, money that could have been saved, prestige, status, income, or the perception of security. But the possibility of loss is also a signpost that what you're doing really matters, that you're vested in both the process and the outcome. Knowing that fuels a deeper commitment to action and to striving not just to create something, but to create something amazing. Risk of loss has to be there. You cannot create genius without having skin in the game. Kill the risk of loss and you destroy meaning and one of the core motivations for action.

It's tough enough to deal with uncertainty, risk, and judgment in the early days of any creative endeavor. Not knowing on day one how it's going to end or what it will look like when it's complete can be paralyzing for many. It's brutally hard to act in the face of incomplete information or assurances that you're on the right path. But it's that very lack of assurance that also serves as proof that the journey you're embarking on is not derivative. That the quest and the potential outcome are unique. That both will matter.

Once you're deeper into an endeavor, how you respond to the realization that your core ideas, hypotheses, and beliefs were dead wrong is often the determining factor in your ability not only to move forward from that point, but to adapt to the information, kick-start a new wave of creativity and innovation, and integrate the lessons from this awakening in a way that allows you to create something even better than, though often radically different from, your initial concept.

In fact, a 2008 study led by Professor Franck Zenasni, published in the *Journal of Creative Behavior*, revealed "tolerance for ambiguity" to be "significantly and positively related" to creativity. Working with a population of parents and their adolescent children, Zenasni and his team measured each participant's creativity using a story-writing task, a divergent-thinking task, and a self-evaluation of creative attitude and behavior. Participants then completed two assessments that measured tolerance for ambiguity. The data revealed a strong link between the creativity and tolerance for ambiguity. Explaining the results, Zenasni argues that tolerance for ambiguity "enables individuals to not be satisfied by partial or non-optimal solutions to complex problems. People who tolerate ambiguity may be able to work effectively on a larger set of stimuli or situations, including ambiguous ones, whereas intolerant individuals will avoid or quickly stop treating such information."

The more you're able to tolerate ambiguity and lean into the unknown, the more likely you'll be to dance with it long enough to come up with better solutions, ideas, and creations.

This finding largely mirrors what we've seen unfold in the lives of the greatest creators and innovators for generations. However, in the context of creativity and innovation, the use of the word "tolerance" is troubling. It frames the experience of uncertainty as one to be endured and suffered rather than invited and embraced as a signpost of opportunity. In the context of creativity and innovation, then, it's more constructive to replace the phrase "tolerance for ambiguity" with "willingness to embrace the unknown."

Some of the greatest innovation and success comes from taking the endeavor a step beyond embracing and downright bum-rushing uncertainty, risk, and criticism.

AMPLIFYING UNCERTAINTY

In mid-2004, a parade of newly minted investment bankers bounced their way down the hallways of two of the most venerable institutions on Wall Street. On paper, that first day, the two groups looked pretty similar: The new bankers, graduates of top schools, were a healthy mix of introverts and extroverts, risk managers and cowboys. All were exceptionally bright, with killer quantitative and analytic skills. All were driven to prove their worth, move up the heavily gilded ladders of power and prestige, do the biggest deals, and make insane amounts of money.

One of those groups was about to be whacked in their heads like never before. And the whacking would last for years. Actually, it would never go away—they'd just learn how to embrace it. Once they did, they'd find themselves able to pull off things that would have left the other group vomiting in the bathroom. They'd develop the ability to solve problems, create and innovate, manage deals, and not only handle but seek out and harness mass levels of uncertainty, levels that would make the average junior banker quake and that would turn the average human into a babbling puddle of anxiety.

The two banks, it turns out, deliberately built their core philosophies, modes of operations, and culture around radically different ideals. For her book *Bullish on Uncertainty* (2009), business professor Alexandra Michel conducted a three-year study of the two banks.

One bank—we'll call it Traditional Bank—was fairly typical of Wall Street institutions. It was built around specific roles and groups, high levels of specialization, best practices, and the quest to identify and extinguish as much uncertainty as possible. When new clients came in, they were pitched by the group leaders: senior bankers with "names" in the industry. Once landed, specialized teams relied largely on the lessons and experiences of the past and established deal analogues to guide how they would create solutions for new clients. Traditional Bank was profitable and the bankers strongly identified with their roles, but they were not known as innovators or market leaders.

The second bank—we'll call them Innovation Bank—couldn't have been more different. Rather than adopting a stance that worked to eliminate uncertainty, the entire firm was built around the idea of intentionally amplifying uncertainty. There were no well-defined roles or groups, no deal analogues, no star players, no standard approaches. New clients were as likely to be pitched by a junior associate as they were to see a senior partner. Once a client was landed, deals weren't staffed by specialized teams, but rather were led by even the most junior bankers, who were charged with "figuring it out" and forced to reach out to and rely on the collective resources of the entire firm. Bankers were told not to look at how similar deals were done in the past, but rather to look at the real-time needs, challenges, and circumstances of the clients, to digest everything, and to come up with the best possible solutions for those clients, given their unique circumstances at that moment in time.

There were no best practices or formal training. It was very much sink or swim. There were no rock stars, since every person was instructed to draw on the combined resources of the firm to assemble a spot team in real time. This approach was designed to deliberately amplify uncertainty, to force bankers to constantly reexamine what they were doing and why, and to keep them from falling into a pattern in which their perception of knowledge, expertise, and prestige blinded them to seeing the needs of any given client at any given time.

At Innovation Bank, certainty was the devil, hubris manifested, the source of big misses and bigger mistakes. It led, according to their philosophy, to people's falling back on the belief that they knew better than the market.

Innovation Bank was known on the street as an innovator, an institution that consistently pushed the envelope, led the market, and was very successful. When times were good, both banks prospered. But as Michel shared with me in an interview, when the market fell apart in 2008 and 2009, Innovation Bank kept humming along. Traditional Bank collapsed under the weight of the market.

What's even more striking than the impact of Innovation Bank's adoption of an amplified uncertainty strategy is the impact it had on the investment bankers themselves. During the first few years, not surprisingly, the Innovation bankers experienced what could only be described as a fair amount of suffering. They lived in an environment defined by constant change and uncertainty, yet they were still evaluated and judged based on their success.

It wasn't unusual for them to report feeling overwhelmed and anxious as they tried to navigate those waters with very little structure. They immediately had to abandon a sense that they could rely on their own abilities and knowledge to get any deal done. Instead, they learned to harness all the resources of the firm and respond with the freshest eyes possible to what was in front of them.

I asked Professor Michel if the reputations of each bank served to preselect applicants based on personality preferences during the hiring process. Not at all, she said. Members of the pool of prospective bankers were remarkably similar before they joined either Traditional or Innovation Bank. But after a few years, the difference was stunning. The environment literally changed not only how the surviving bankers thought, but how they solved problems, identified themselves, accrued ego, and remained open to input in the quest to create the best possible outcome.

When people left Traditional Bank, they would generally go to a similar position in another bank. That was what they knew and what they were groomed for. When people left Innovation Bank, many left the field entirely, having gained not only a deep knowledge of banking, but an additional universe of skills and a mind-set that prepared them not just to thrive as bankers, but to be able to create extraordinary outcomes in nearly any setting or industry.

EXALTING UNCERTAINTY

On a Friday evening in 1997 at the University of Manchester, esteemed scientist Andre Geim was busy at work. The project at hand? Levitating frogs.

Not to be outdone, in 2003 Geim and fellow researcher Konstantin Novoselov turned their Friday evenings to the work of creating "gecko tape," micro-engineered tape that mimics the physics geckos use to adhere to nearly any surface. Proof of concept came in the form of a Spiderman action figure dangling from the ceiling, adhered only by a tiny piece of the gecko tape that, according to the researchers, could allow a human being the same experience. Sadly, though many in the lab volunteered to test the theory by hanging on the wall outside the lab building, Geim and Novoselov had trouble justifying the large amount of money it would have taken to create enough tape to humanize the experiment.

Both "scientific diversions" came out of what Geim and Novoselov refer to as their Friday evening experiments, where they, in Novoselov's words:

> just do all kinds of crazy things that probably won't pan out at all, but if they do, it would be really surprising. Geim did frog levitation as one of these experiments, and then we did gecko tape together. There are many more that were unsuccessful and never went anywhere (though I still had a good time thinking about and doing those experiments, so I love them no less than the successful ones).

If this sounds like folly for a lab renowned for extraordinary research and endowed with a healthy stream of funding for "serious" work, think again. Out of these same Friday evening experiments came a series of discoveries about a substance called graphene—a single layer of graphite strong enough to build a hammock for a cat that would weigh as little as a whisker—that landed the pair the Nobel Prize in 2010.

At around the same time Geim and Novoselov were creating superhuman adhesives and hover-frogs, some 6,000 miles away on a sprawling campus in northern California, former Google employee number 23, Paul Buchheit, was busy at work on a seemingly equally crazy idea. He was creating a browser-based, free e-mail service that would scan e-mails and serve up ads related to the content of the message. The entire thing was coded in a day, though it would take years and many iterations before Buchheit's Gmail would grow into one of Google's biggest successes and most pervasively used products.

In its infancy, the product was filled with bugs and controversy, and it could have easily been killed. But it fell under what Google calls its 20% time, a core tenet of Google's philosophy that says employees are not only allowed but expected to allocate 20% of their time, or a day a week, to projects that interest them. This allocation of time has led to the creation of a number of Google's biggest products and profit centers, and has driven a mass expansion of users and resulted in billions in annual revenue.

As Buchheit shared on his blog in January 2009:

> If you want innovation, it's critical that people are able to work on ideas that are unapproved and generally thought to be stupid. The real value of "20%" is not the time, but rather the "license" it gives to work on things that "aren't important."

The power of Geim and Novoselov's Friday evening experiments and Google's 20% time is not that they're permitted, but rather that they are baked into the core ideals and philosophy of the organizations. They are public statements that tell all the employees that taking risks, trying nutty things, and leaning into uncertainty will be met with acceptance, regardless of the outcomes, and will be an essential part of what they're there to do.

IT'S NOT JUST FOR START-UPS AND TECH

That's all well and good, you may say, for labs and organizations that are in the business of innovation, but what about real companies that create "real" products and services? What about more established retailers whose customers tend to be far less forgiving of experimentation and inconsistency?

Starbucks is a great example. Nobody wants their morning latte messed with. For years, former Starbucks International president Howard Behar, along with Howard Shultz and Orin Smith, formed a powerhouse governing trio, known internally as H2O, that helped drive the Starbucks brand from a few dozen stores to a worldwide experiential retail behemoth.

Starbucks is known in the retail consumer product and experience world as a true innovator. But in the early days they were a very different business. Their focus was so narrow and they were so determined to keep it that way that the Frappuccino brand almost never came to be.

Dina Campion was one of the first Starbucks district managers in Southern California. She noticed that Starbucks' competitors were selling a beverage that her stores didn't have, so she asked Behar to come down and try the frozen coffee treat. He did, liked it, and figured if they made their own version they could sell about thirty a day in their stores. At the time, that would have represented a 5% bump in average store volume.

So Behar went back to Seattle and said, "Hey, we've got to do this."

There was a resounding "no" vote from the team. "We don't do that at Starbucks," they said. "We're in the coffee business." He called Campion with the bad news, and she asked if she could test out the beverage in her stores anyway. Behar knew he was going against the whole team but gave her the go-ahead anyway, and the sales were remarkable. Once again, Behar presented the new beverage to the team, and this time Schultz approved a ninety-day test. That one hard-fought experiment has now turned into a multibillion-dollar-a-year product line.

The real challenge with experimenting in a retail operation like Starbucks is that, unlike tech companies that are explicitly in the business of creating new things, retail businesses want sameness and consistency. They don't want imperfection—the people they're serving want to be sure that every time they go into a Starbucks store, wherever they order, it's exactly the same.

Still, even in that highly controlled environment, you need to give some room to uncertainty. Behar calls it "texture," adding, "that's when the good stuff comes. It's when people are fooling around. And then you've got to be able to figure out how to harvest that stuff, how to listen to it."

Inviting the unknown isn't just for tortured solo creators. Even in the biggest, most established retailers, it is the lifeblood of innovation.

HAILED BUT REVILED

Linguistics aside, this much is clear. The ability not only to endure but to invite, amplify, and exalt uncertainty, then reframe it as fuel is paramount to your ability to succeed as a creator. Visionary innovation and creativity cannot happen when every variable, every outcome, every permutation is known and has been tested and validated in advance. You cannot see the world differently if it's already been seen in every possible way. You cannot solve a problem better if every solution has already been defined. You cannot create great art if every way to stroke a canvas, connect a note, or grace a stage has already been inventoried, categorized, and laid bare for all to see. If everything is known and certain, that means it's all been done before. And creation isn't about repetition.

Genius always starts with a question, not an answer. Eliminate the question and you eliminate the possibility of genius. However, that's where things get really sticky. For all but a rare few, "living in the question" hurts. It causes anxiety, fear, suffering, and pain. And people don't like pain. Rather than lean into it, we do everything possible to snuff it out. Not because we have to, but because we can't handle the discomfort that we assume "has to" go along with the quest. Snuffing out uncertainty leads to a sea of prematurely terminated mediocre output, when that "sweet mother of God" breakthrough was just over the hump if only we'd had the will to embrace uncertainty, risk, and judgment and hang on a bit longer. If only we'd learned how to harness and ride rather than hunt and kill the butterflies that live in the gut of every person who strives to create something extraordinary from nothing.

2

WHAT UNCERTAINTY DOES TO US

IF IT'S SO obvious that embracing uncertainty, risk, and criticism is essential for high-level creativity and innovation, why do so many people who have the drive to create run in the other direction the moment they feel these signposts of creation touching down? It turns out that, without intervention, a blend of nature and nurture conspire to make us experience these elements as suffering.

PICK AN URN, ANY URN

Back in 1961, Daniel Ellsberg became fascinated with the difference between risk and uncertainty. In the world of economics, people were always working on ways to quantify risk and fold it into equations and approaches that could help manage it. Ellsberg saw risk as a bit of a red herring, because in real life we are far more likely to face scenarios in which there is risk, but it's simply not quantifiable—moments of great uncertainty when both the magnitude and the probability of success or failure cannot be determined in advance.

How do you calculate your personal odds of succeeding as an artist or the value people will place on a radical new group of paintings you're working on? How do you define the heights to which you might rise or fall as an entrepreneur, writer, or actor? What's the risk associated with wearing your heart on your sleeve and being rejected, or with creating art, music, or a business for which there are no analogues? It's one thing to weigh odds and magnitudes in the laboratory. In the real world, it's not so easy.

Ellsberg realized that most of life, including a good number of the biggest decisions we make, requires action in the face of risk that is not definable, that is uncertain. Actually, of all variables, the easiest to quantify is often the magnitude and impact of failure, which is one of the reasons our brains tend to spiral into that abyss. But the odds and magnitude of success are near impossible to define. Still, you need to take action in the face of what is often incomplete information and great uncertainty.

Ellsebrg wanted to gain a better understanding of how this uncertainty affected the decisions people make and the actions they take, so he devised a fascinating experiment. Imagine walking into a room to find a table with two urns on it. The urn on the left contains 100 balls, 50 white and 50 black. The urn on the right also contains 100 black and white balls, but the percentage of each color is unknown. You learn that a single ball will be drawn from one of the urns and you'll have to bet $100 on which color it will be. You're then asked to choose which of the two urns you want the ball drawn from.

Think about it. Which urn would you choose?

If you choose the one with 50 white and 50 black balls, welcome to the club. Apparently, you're human. Most people make that choice.

Mathematically and logically, there is no reason to choose the

50/50 urn over the other. But in an experiment Ellsberg oversaw, that's exactly what most people did. This experiment, which yielded what is known as the Ellsberg paradox, has been repeated in a wide variety of formats and settings over fifty years, always with the same result. People steer away from the uncertain option.

On a visceral, "can't explain why" level, most people don't like uncertainty. Actually, that's an understatement. Most people run like hell from it, even when there's no rational reason to prefer a known option over an ambiguous or uncertain one. The Ellsberg paradox is a stunning indictment of our inability to handle action in the face of uncertainty. But these experiments also left a giant lingering question: Why?

Why are we so terrified of the unknown?

For years, the answer was subject to a wide variety of hypotheses, but recent magnetic resonance imaging studies on subjects undergoing the Ellsberg paradox trials add clarity. The aversion to uncertainty, it seems, is hardwired into most people. When exposed to the urn with an unknown mix of balls, a part of the brain known as the amygdala, which is a core instigator of fear and anxiety, lights up, triggering a cascade of physiological and psychological events, sending impulses and chemicals rushing through our bodies that induce a state of hyperalertness and, for many, anywhere from mild to severe fear and anxiety.

This action of the amygdala makes most people experience uncertainty not as something to be desired and danced with but as a form of suffering to be banished by any means necessary. Most of us—not all of us, and not all on the same level—but most of us react to uncertainty strongly enough for it to be a limiting factor in our lives and in our willingness to act in the face of it. If we look a bit deeper, though, we see that neurologically driven primal resistance to uncertainty isn't the only roadblock.

UNCERTAINTY AND JUDGMENT

Uncertainty and fear of judgment go hand in hand. The more you lean into uncertainty and the greater the risks you take to create something that didn't exist before, the greater will be the potential for you to be judged and criticized. That judgment is almost always served up as a three-layer cake:

- *Judgment from those whose approval you seek*—peers, mentors, students, family, friends, current investors or your board, competitors, thought leaders, and media influencers.
- *Judgment from those whose money you seek in exchange for your creations*—potentially all of the above, plus customers, venture capitalists, angels, lenders, and patrons.
- *Judgment from yourself.* Even if you never dare to release your creation into the wild, it still comes from inside.

The judgment is all wrapped around two big questions that all creators constantly wrestle with, especially in those critical creation crux moments:

Is *this* good enough?

Am *I* good enough?

We are often terrified of getting answers to those questions we don't want to hear. This aversion to being judged, to being told something doesn't measure up, leads so many to either cut creative quests short or, worse, never even begin. It's molasses in the machine of creation.

That alone is a tough enough challenge for the creative soul who typically spends a good chunk of time pining for acceptance. But the effect can actually be far more insidious. It extends beyond slowing down the *pace* of creation and impacts the *amplitude* of innovation by making you less tolerant of uncertainty and, in turn, either less innovative or less willing to share what may be perceived as loony ideas with others.

THE JUDGMENT AND UNCERTAINTY DEATH SPIRAL

Recall the Ellsberg paradox. Given the chance to pick an urn and wager on the color of the ball, most people picked the urn with the known balance of balls, based on no rational reason. They exhibited very little tolerance for uncertainty, and that, as we've noted, can have the effect of functionally capping creativity and innovation. But that wasn't the end of the story.

The subjects in the experiment all knew they were being watched and judged based on the choice they made. In the face of the potential for public scrutiny, most went for the urn with a known distribution of balls. In 2008 though, researchers Stefan T. Trautmann, Ferdinand M. Vieider, and Peter P. Wakker wondered what might happen if they removed the expectation of judgment from the experiment. Would that change the subjects' tolerance for ambiguity and uncertainty? Would it make them more open to the choice with the less certain outcome?

To find out, the team replicated variations of the Ellsberg experiment but created a scenario in which the subjects could participate and potentially win a prize without being concerned about ever having to reveal their choices. In their report of the experiment, the researchers noted, "Remarkably, *eliminating the possibility of evaluation by others makes ambiguity aversion disappear entirely*. . . . Introducing the possibility of evaluation . . . is sufficient to make ambiguity aversion reemerge as strongly as commonly found." (italics added)

In this experiment, Trautmann's team revealed how our pervasive inability to tolerate ambiguity and uncertainty isn't just about the brain's hardwiring for survival, as had often been assumed. That's a major factor. But there's something else big at play. There is a substantial social context to it.

We'll create with abandon, make bolder choices, lean into uncertainty, and take risks far more readily if we know that whatever comes out of that effort will never be revealed to others. The moment we introduce the element of exposure, judgment, criticism, and the potential for rejection, most people run for the certainty fences. And in doing so, they become less willing to push boundaries, take risks, and choose less-certain options that often yield the greatest opportunities.

The fallout of that, for creators in any field, is creative output that's not what it could have been (a) had it been done without the advance expectation of being judged or (b) had we developed the tools not just to be okay with the prospect of being judged, but to extract knowledge from judgment and leverage it to improve our creations.

In reality, we may not be as hardwired to avoid uncertainty as we are hardwired to avoid wanting to be judged for taking the less-mainstream path and coming up empty. Fear of judgment stifles our ability to embrace uncertainty and as part of that process delivers a serious blow to our willingness to create anything that hasn't already been done and validated.

This very phenomenon has been shown numerous times in the work of Harvard creativity researcher Teresa Amabile. In one experiment, Amabile collected 20 completed works from each of 23 artists; half of the works by each artist were commissioned, meaning there was a clear expectation of public evaluation and judgment from the get-go, and half were created with no expectation that they'd ever see the light of day. All 460 works were then evaluated for creativity by a panel of experts that included gallery owners, art historians, museum curators, and others. None knew the identity of the artists nor whether any given work was commissioned or not.

With great surprise, Amabile reported, "The commissioned works were rated as significantly less creative than the non-commissioned works, yet they were not rated as different in technical quality." While part of that loss in creativity may be due to a shift from intrinsic to extrinsic motivation (soul work versus paid work), Trautmann's work shows that the change in the artists' expectations of exposure, evaluation, and judgment likely plays a very real, if not predominant, role in the drop in creativity.

The studies done by Trautmann's team and by Amabile paint a fascinating picture of the impact of fear of judgment on our tolerance for ambiguity, uncertainty, risk taking, and creativity.

Exposure to judgment and uncertainty aren't going away. Nor, as a creator, do you want them to. Judgment, delivered constructively, provides the information needed to create at higher and higher levels. And uncertainty is a signpost of novelty and innovation, telling you that what you're creating is really worth creating.

For most other endeavors, once that energy cedes to the more long-term, "get it done" nature of any meaningful creative endeavor, the discomfort and anxiety that ride along become a stronger and stronger force.

All too often, one of two things happens. The fear and anxiety lure you into wanting to move too quickly from freedom to constraint. They make you want to close off options, create rules, systems, and processes, stop exploring, adapting, testing, permuting, experimenting, and evolving. Not because it's the right time, not because you've finally reached a point at which you've accomplished what you're truly capable of, but because the uncertainty, the anxiety, the suffering that comes from not being "there" yet or from fear of being criticized for taking a risk and getting it wrong is killing you. And you just want it to end.

Or the opposite happens. Your inability to wrangle the fear and uncertainty stops you from ever starting or makes you so freaked out about making the wrong decisions that you endlessly debate every step along the way, lose your ability to make decisions and take action, and end up stalled.

The move from freedom to constraint has to happen. If it doesn't, there's no output . . . and no impact. The key is to hit that sweet spot, giving yourself enough time to play in the realm of possibilities before yielding to the limits and structures needed to execute on your best ideas.

Even when a particular project—be it a painting, book, product, service, or entity—comes into being, that's only part of a much bigger creation journey. When you broaden your view, such endeavors become stopping points, snapshots of your capabilities and your contribution to a much bigger quest to build a body of work or a meaningful career over a lifetime. Each endeavor is a giant creation crux move on a far grander creation arc that will take decades to build.

One of the biggest awakenings as you strive to build a project, a career, and a life worthy of a legacy is that, in the end, there is no there there. No resting point. No certainty. No place to hide from either the inner or outer critics. The book may be finished, the movie wrapped, the company launched, or the product revealed. But what will you do when you go to work tomorrow?

You and what you create will remain, to varying degrees, in a state of constant evolution. If you're properly equipped to handle "living in the question," that's not a bad thing. Your ability not only to live with but lean into and proactively seek out risk, judgment, and uncertainty—to transform it from what is, for most people, a default experience of suffering into fuel for creation—will play a huge role in your ability to create genius in every aspect of your work, your relationships, and your life, both in the moment and over a lifetime.

The question is whether this is possible. If we are hardwired to run from uncertainty, risk, and judgment and if those things are mandatory elements of creation, are we creators just royally screwed? Are we just genetically encoded to suffer in the name of our art? Or are there things we can change that might allow us to embrace the uncertainty, risk, and judgment needed for high-level creation? Given the right approach, can anyone figure out how to dissociate just enough from the fear and anxiety to make the journey more humane and actually enjoyable?

3

THE MYTH OF THE FEARLESS CREATOR

IN 1990 JOHN Winsor acquired the rights to publish *Women's Sports & Fitness*, which was then hanging on by a thread. Battling what from the outside appeared to be ridiculous odds, within three years he'd turned the magazine around and added more titles. He then sold the company to Condé Nast in 1998 and launched a new venture, a marketing firm called Radar Communications, with Nike as a starting client. Nine years later, he sold Radar to Crispin, Porter + Bogusky, where he'd serve as VP/Executive Director of Strategy and Innovation before launching Victors & Spoils, a new agency built around a highly controversial and provocative crowd-sourcing strategy. Winsor, it seems, is in constant creation and evolution mode, always riding the edge.

When he's not in his office, he's often out surfing big waves, helicopter skiing, or rock climbing. With his seeming ability to repeatedly embrace endeavors defined by what for most would be crushing levels of uncertainty, risk, and exposure, some might wonder if he's simply a neurological anomaly, gifted with a brain that doesn't feel fear or anxiety. The exact opposite is true.

He feels it intensely, but experiences it differently. For Winsor, it's not about tempting fate, it's about going to that place where magic happens. "When the risks are big," Winsor shared with me, "it's where I feel most alive. In a weird way, it's almost a meditative thing. When a lot's on the line, whether it's a big business deal or surfing a scary wave, I get so focused. Things slow down. The tiniest of details become alive, the feeling of a pebble beneath your shoe on a rock wall or the real meaning of a sentence in a business deal." That experience, to Winsor, is what it's all about. Rather than deterring action, he's figured out how to experience it as the place from which the greatest opportunities arise. Indeed, the very activities he engages in, especially outside of work, and the consistency with which he undertakes them may be at the root of his ability to experience scenarios that would paralyze others as opportunities to go deeper.

It's the same with *Perfect Storm* (1997) and *War* (2010) author Sebastian Junger. In a 2010 interview with *Outside* magazine, he revealed a similar ability to lean into great waves of fear and uncertainty in the name of telling powerful stories. At the time, Junger was recently back from being embedded with a platoon of U.S. soldiers in Afghanistan's Korengal Valley that came under attack on a regular basis. His book *War* and documentary film *Restrepo* (2010) came out of that experience.

With everything Junger commits to, he assumes he's going to fail. "I'm very scared of failure," he shared in *Outside* magazine, ". . . and that sense of impossibility gets me to crank up the turbines. Everything mentally and physically at my disposal I pour into a project."

Junger's seeming ability to harness the fear that cripples so many other creators, especially writers, is something that's been with him for as long as he can remember. In a later conversation with me, he revealed, "I just figured out how to disengage from my experience of the fear and I do that with a lot of different emotions. I can do it with anger, frustration, whatever. I start feeling it and then I could just unhook from it. . . . I was a climber for tree companies and I'm scared of heights, but I never got over my fear of heights. I just figured out how to not think about it. It was really simple."

Winsor and Junger are examples of top creators in their fields, men who innovate and craft a near-endless stream of enviable output. They have found ways to frame and experience fear as just another name for intense attention and motivation, a necessary component of any serious creative effort. Both have been doing it for as long as they can remember.

What's automatic at this point for Winsor and Junger is brutally hard for most creators. Their ability to turn fear from a paralytic force into a vital fuel is likely one of the key determinants in their ability to create on a level most others aspire to yet never attain. Which makes you wonder—do some people touch down on the planet with the innate ability to handle fear and anxiety, especially in the context of great quests, more easily than everyone else? Is this something you either have or don't have? Or can it be acquired through training?

TRAINING IN THE ALCHEMY OF FEAR

What if, unlike John Winsor and Sebastian Junger, you lust after the quest to create but have not yet discovered how to lean into fear? What if the uncertainty, risk, and exposure to judgment that give rise to fear and anxiety make you want not to create but to vomit? What if it shuts you and your creative quests down? Can you teach yourself to be a fear alchemist and, in doing so, develop the ability to tap into the fuel side of fear to create on a whole different level?

Many creators and innovators feel called to create but are not well equipped to handle the angst of doing it on a high level over a sustained period of time. Because of this, many walk away from the call, trading creation for calm. But others end up building risk, exposure, and uncertainty "scaffolding." They adopt practices and structures around the way they work and how they live in the world that allow them to cultivate enough head space and baseline calm to keep pushing the envelope of creation without losing their minds. Like the fabled medieval alchemists, who were said to be equipped with a secret elixir that turned everyday metals into gold, these creators train themselves to transform uncertainty, fear, and doubt into fuel for creation. They become fear alchemists, often without even realizing what they're doing.

The balance of this book is an exploration of these practices and changes in environment and process.

We will explore the role of certainty anchors, a hidden aspect of the ritual and routine that underpin both the creative and the everyday activities of so many of the world's greatest innovators and creators. We will also see how ritual plays a secondary role in fortifying creators against the aspects of the creative process that, at least earlier in their journeys, are more repulsive than engaging.

We will look at creative hives and explore the dynamic that unfolds when you either find or cultivate your own constructive, judgment-leveling collectives of like-minded creators. We'll also see what happens when emotional contagion turns constructive energy bad and the dynamic goes awry. And we will lay out a set of guidelines designed to aid in the quest to help create or find the right setting and people.

We will dive into the rapidly evolving world of technology and see how platforms that have become broadly available only in the last few years are creating opportunities to change the creative process. These technologies are affecting the psychology of creation in a profound way by allowing for rapid, affordable prototyping, feedback, and user co-creation. We'll explore how these technologies can extend into the realms of even traditional solo creators and artists and into nontechnical fields. We will also examine how, without intelligent, creative leadership, these same technologies can allow the creation process to become co-opted, diluted, and even bastardized, yielding watered-down output and taking advantage of participants in the process.

We will explore the role of mentors, heroes, and champions, looking at how the involvement of each can accelerate the creation process and how the overreliance on each also holds the potential to paralyze the process. We will also do a bit of myth busting along the way.

From there, we'll turn our energies toward daily personal practices that, over time, will transform the way you experience the uncertainty, risk, and exposure of the creation process and that will allow you to lean into those challenges with enough zest to create on a different level—and do so with more equanimity and less pain. We will look at how attentional training relieves much of the dark side while simultaneously jacking your creative and cognitive abilities through the roof.

We'll reexamine the role of visualization in the context of the creator's journey, debunking the most popular method and exploring a much more powerful alternative approach. We will see how a single shift in the way we define what's possible can make a profound impact on our willingness to embrace the uncertainty, risk, and exposure needed to fuel the work that drives extraordinary achievement. And we'll look at the practice of reframing, especially in the context of the risk of "extreme loss," and gain an understanding of how to use this tool to change the stories that guide our efforts.

We'll dive into one of the greatest practical challenges every committed creator must face: the never-ending tension between the near-addictive pull of your own muse and the desire to honor the people, activities, and commitments that make your pursuit of creative genius possible yet might be cast aside as collateral lifestyle damage along the way. We'll look at how the very same practices that help manage uncertainty can be leveraged to help manage those often at-odds desires.

Finally, we will explore one of the hardest decisions any creator must make: when to push an endeavor forward or shut it down. And we'll lay out a set of questions and guidelines to help you understand whether the little voice that says "I'm done" is just resistance that should be pushed aside or intelligence that should rule the day.

Onward then, to the world of the fear alchemist.

4

FIND YOUR CERTAINTY ANCHORS

FROM THE DAWN of religion, nearly every faith has been built around not just scripture, not just community, but ritual. Hindus give offerings every morning. Buddhists chant and meditate. Christians receive communion and hold and count rosaries. Jews experience bat and bar mitzvahs, and many live by the rules of Kashrut. Muslims gather facing Mecca and pray five times a day. Members of many faiths recite the same prayers every day and share a weekly break, a Sabbath ritual, seasonal rites, or common rules about how to live and behave and treat others.

For many, especially those of deep faith, there is intense meaning and a sense of grounding connected to these faith-based rituals.

But if you strip away the beliefs and leave only the underlying rituals, you may be surprised to discover that rituals alone still have immense power as tools to counter the anxieties of an uncertain life. They may not be as powerful as rituals anchored to faith, but a significant part of what is going on with rituals occurs in a realm beyond beliefs.

Why? Because the simple physical act of engaging in ritual and routine serves as a certainty anchor.

THE POWER OF CERTAINTY ANCHORS

A certainty anchor is a practice or process that adds something known and reliable to your life when you may otherwise feel you're spinning off in a million different directions. Rituals and routines can function as certainty anchors by offering a sense of connection with the divine or with a like-minded community. A lot of the power of rituals and routines comes from the simple fact that they are always there. They are grounding experiences to which you can always return, no matter what's going on. Their consistency makes them effective tools to counter the anxiety that comes not only from living in uncertain times, but from embracing endeavors that ramp uncertainty even higher.

For the creator, whose very existence depends on the ability to spend vast amounts of time living and operating in the ethereal sea of uncertainty and anxiety that is creation, rituals in every part of life serve as a source of psychic bedrock. They provide just enough of a foundation to allow you to free up that part of your brain that needs permission to run unencumbered in the quest to create the greatest possible something from nothing.

Some of the most creative people in the world are attached to rituals and routines in their everyday lives. Novelist CJ Lyons has taken most of her mundane daily tasks, from laundry to lunch, and dropped them into a routine that hasn't been altered in years. Professional blogger Darren Rowse starts each day by heading off to his favorite café, ostensibly to find a good place to write, but there's a lot of ritual in that as well. Joe Fig's fascinating look at the daily routines of artists,

Inside the Painter's Studio (2009), reveals that many of them maintain a near-dogged attachment to daily routine. For example, the artist Ross Bleckner has for years kept to the same standardized day from the moment he opens his eyes to the moment he goes to sleep, seven days a week.

In her classic book *The Creative Habit* (2003), legendary choreographer Twyla Tharp shares how she would awaken at 5:30 a.m. every day, take a taxi to the gym, work out with the same trainer, shower, eat three hard-boiled egg whites and coffee, make calls for one hour, work in her studio for two hours, rehearse with her company, return home for dinner, read for a few hours, then go to bed. Every day, the same routine. "A dancer's life," she said, "is all about repetition."

Commenting on the role of certainty anchors in his life, Steven Pressfield, whose book *The War of Art* (2002) opens a window into the power of ritual in creative work, shared with me his belief that to be a writer is to live in total insecurity. You never know where your next job is coming from, you never know if the next thing you do is going to find a market. "So . . . let's say managing my money," he offered, "I'm the most conservative person in the world. I just give it to a friend who takes care of everything for me. The only place I take risks is in the work. And then that's where I feel like your job is to take risks."

Broader lifestyle routines serve as a salve to calm a bit of the anxiety of creation and to drop an anchor to which we can tether our creative lines, knowing we can then float higher up into the clouds and stay there longer, trusting that we'll be able to find our way down.

Rituals within the narrower creation process have other, less obvious benefits. They help overcome the fear, anxiety, and discomfort that comes from embracing the part of the work that tends to antagonize you, but not for the reasons most people think. To understand what's really happening here, we need to dive deeper into the phases of creation and the starting preferences of creators.

THE TWO PHASES OF CREATION

Creation unfolds in two fairly distinct phases:

- Insight/Dot Connecting/Disruption
- Refinement, Expansion, and Production (REP)

Though often intertwined in an almost indiscernible fabric, each of these phases has its own unique drivers and challenges.

INSIGHT/DOT CONNECTING/DISRUPTION

In her TED talk in February 2009, *Eat, Pray, Love* author Elizabeth Gilbert told a story about an American poet named Ruth Stone. When Stone was out in the fields working, according to Gilbert, "She said she would feel and hear a poem coming at her from over the landscape. And she said it was like a thunderous train of air. And it would come barreling down at her over the landscape." Many creators in both business and art share variations, though they are often less graphic, on the experience of receiving what they describe as flashes of insight, gifts from the muse, or revelations—moments during which exceptional ideas, syntheses, and awakenings seem to come to them, often at the most inconvenient times and not infrequently when they're off the official "working" clock.

I've experienced this thousands of times, as an entrepreneur, a writer, a painter, and a musician. Books, headlines, product ideas, solutions to giant problems, riffs, and images seem to simply arrive. The name for my last company, Sonic Yoga, dropped from the sky a few years before I even knew what to do with it. I just knew I had to reserve the URL because the idea for something worth experiencing would somehow find its way into existence and wrap its way around the name. Sentences or at times entire paragraphs have an odd habit of creeping into my mind when I'm in the middle of long drives or six-mile hikes, without a pen to be found.

Steven Johnson, author of *Where Good Ideas Come From* (2010), spent years researching how these flashes of insight occur. The "perception" of a momentary experience of revelation, he suggests, is a bit misguided. Rather, big, disruptive ideas tend to evolve as what he calls "slow hunches," rumblings that build over years and sometimes even decades until they bump into other people and ideas. That collision triggers the recombination of information, provokes new points of view, and stimulates the release of new, bigger ideas, formulations, revelations, and syntheses. These recombined and new ideas are experienced as momentary awakenings, but in reality the pieces of the big idea have been percolating for quite a while. They just needed to find the other pieces that would unlock the wisdom hidden inside.

While I've experienced flashes of creative insight through the collision of ideas, I have also been struck by creative lightning through the vehicle of contemplation, often in isolation. So I do believe that Johnson's collision of ideas can serve as an incendiary device for big ideas, but I also see the exact opposite: for me, downtime or seemingly nonproductive, noninteractive, noncreative space often results in a great tilling of soil that yields big ideas. There's something powerful about working hard, then stepping away and doing things that calm your mental chatter enough to create space for the big ideas to arise.

The insight phase of the creation process is big, potentially disruptive, and raw, fraught with tragic flaws and wild opportunities in equal measure. It's the moment when a breathless plot twist or stunning resolution occurs to a fiction writer, when the image of a scene, filled with color, light, and movement, forms in the mind's eye of a painter, when the code that makes everything work comes to a developer, when the solution to a nagging problem occurs to an enterprising entrepreneur.

Those bursts are capable of generating a huge amount of creative heat and fueling more work. As we'll see a bit later, they can also literally infect others with emotion and energy. But they're also almost always in need of a lot of help.

To get from the moment of insight to a finished book, painting, platform, solution, or business, that insight needs to be refined, expanded, and produced (REP)—and, often, radically altered. That's where the REP phase of creation comes in.

REFINE, EXPAND, PRODUCE (REP)

REP is all about building out, testing, expanding, refining, detailing, debugging, and improving big ideas and insights. For entrepreneurs, it's where the visionary individual generally ends up butting heads with the operations and process people charged with turning the idea into something executable and profitable. The incremental, methodical, process-oriented nature of building out the big idea is something that tends to suck the life out of most of those who self-identify as big idea people, founders, or visionaries. And the thought of a blank white page often terrifies those who say they are more REP-oriented.

Insight and REP are not just phases within the creation process; they also represent two very distinct personal creative orientations. Your own orientation is defined not so much by what you're good at, but by what energizes you.

It is interesting that society tends to label those with an orientation toward insight as "creatives," while those with an orientation toward

REP—like accountants, bankers, and other quantitative or process-oriented creators—are viewed as noncreative professionals.

The truth is, we all create all the time, in business and in life. It's the way we are most comfortable manifesting those creative juices, through insight or through REP, that differentiates us. According to California Leadership Center founder Bryan Franklin, if you have the benefit of working with a team, there's a huge benefit to having both types of creators in the room together. It's often exposure, even if grudgingly endured, to the REP side of the process that serves up enough raw data or creates enough opportunity for Steven Johnson's collision of ideas to trigger the next big insight. When you put insight creators and REP creators in a room together, each orientation feeds off the work of the other. The end result often exceeds what either type could create independently. Insight and REP are like the yin and yang of creation.

Here's where we circle back to the power of ritual and routine as certainty anchors in the creation process. Knowing your creative orientation is the key to unlocking how and why ritual really works its magic within the context of the creation process. Let's look at these preferences in more detail.

RITUAL, RESISTANCE, AND CREATIVE ORIENTATION

When you are left to do the work that aligns most closely with your creative orientation and when you are bolstered by the practices we'll explore later in the book, you don't really have a need for extraordinary structure. You don't need ritual or routine as a "stick" or vehicle to force you to do your work, because the work you're doing is what you feel you're here to do. It may take effort, but it energizes you, so you're pulled toward it, and there's no need for a push.

If you have the benefit of a team or organization to work with, it's important to have people in the mix who represent both orientations. If you don't, you'll either end up with a room full of people thundering out ideas and looking for someone to do something with them, or a room full of people who are waiting for someone to give them a big idea or starting point to work with.

But what if you don't have a team?

What if you're a solo creator and it's all up to you? What if you have to play the roles of both the big idea person and the REP person, regardless of your orientation, experience, and abilities?

That is the very situation most artists and entrepreneurs find themselves in. It's the rare solo creator or small-team member who gets to pick and choose only the part of the process they are organically drawn to—the one that fills them up and that they've built mad skills around. Most people end up forced to wade into the waters of the creative role that makes them uncomfortable—the side of the process where they've spent far less time and feel far less capable. This is where fear and anxiety creep into the process, tempting you to avoid doing work you feel less equipped to handle, work you would much prefer to be able to pay someone else to slog through.

When I launched my last company, I was an idea terrorist. Every two seconds, I'd have a new idea about what we were going to do, how we'd define the brand, whom we'd serve, what kind of lighting we'd have, the type of music we'd create, the people we'd hire, what they'd wear, the tiles in the bathrooms. If I could get paid to do just that—letting my people figure out how to craft my ideas into viable businesses, books, events, and experiences—I'd be in heaven.

I don't like details, minutiae, process. Baby steps slay me. Systems development makes me cry. Fleshing out, editing, and incremental progress give me hives. But as a bootstrap entrepreneur and a writer, I haven't had a choice. I've had amazing teams to help, but in the end, I've always been responsible for the bulk of both parts of the process (and that has absolutely nothing to do with the fact that I'm a control freak who doesn't trust anyone else to do justice to the purported glory that's blending around in my head).

I don't like having to take on the REP side of creation. It makes me uncomfortable, anxious, uncertain. While I know it's necessary, my immediate experience of the REP side of the process is more emptying than filling. When I'm forced to live on the REP side of the street, I have to fight hard not to shut down.

This is the place where resistance lives: where you are forced to face the part of creation that comes hardest to you.

In real-life applications, the line between the two phases gets blurred. When I conceive, then plan, stage, launch, and grow a businesses or project, I flit constantly between the two states. It's the same thing when I write. Over the course of 250 pages, I toggle between insight and REP thousands of times, with each state often lasting only minutes or seconds. When I'm rocking ideas and insights, you couldn't pay me enough to stop what I'm doing. This is the part of the process that's near addictive. When I'm tasked with fleshing out, expanding, refining, and producing those ideas, it's Twitter time.

This is where ritual and routine, done right, add immense power to the process. Ritual helps train you to sit down when you most want to stand, when you're forced to work on the part of the process that leaves you anywhere from bored to riddled with anxiety.

Over time, ritual has a funny side effect. It creates momentum. It becomes a habit that builds its own head of steam, one capable of overriding the call of Twitter, Facebook, Green & Black's Dark 85% chocolate, and trying to learn whether the rumors about Apple's next product are true.

It fortifies you against Pressfield's resistance and Seth Godin's lizard brain. That alone is a huge benefit for any creator. But there's something else happening under the imposition of ritual law that bears discussion.

Over time, through sheer force of practice, you begin to get better at the side of the process that empties you out. Maybe never as good as someone whose creative orientation pulls them toward it, but good enough to be better than most others who don't work as hard at it as you do. Better than you thought you'd ever be at it. And when that happens, you begin to experience that side of the dance with greater tolerance. The distaste and anxiety diminishes just enough to make you no longer hate it. Repeated exposure to it reduces your fear of it.

Though it's still not fun, the part of your psyche that kept taunting you with how bad you were at it begins to back down. Because you may not like it, but even you've got to admit you've become pretty good at it. The loathing begins to cede to a kinder acceptance that this is just part of what you need to do to create the work you need to create. There may even come a time when you develop a level of mastery over that part of the process, which begins to draw you, in a way you never imagined possible, toward it.

We all hate doing what we're bad at. Mastery may not be enough to offset your creative orientation, but, given time, it often solves enough of the discomfort to turn the hatred into appeasement. That shift alone is huge.

While ritual can play a big role in moving the creative process forward throughout an endeavor, its impact is likely the greatest as you close in on your goal.

Especially if you do it the way The Energy Project founder and author Tony Schwartz does it.

RITUAL, WILLPOWER, AND THE FINAL PUSH

When writing his most recent book, *Be Excellent at Anything* (2010), Schwartz structured his day into three ninety-minute writing bursts that allowed him to complete the book working only four and a half hours a day for three months. Our brains, Schwartz discovered, become easily fatigued. They need breaks in order to refuel, to be able to refocus, create, and produce. When we don't give them the needed time to refuel, they more or less start to shut down and ratchet up the mood crank factor until we have to listen. By then we've often spent hours *at* work, without actually *accomplishing* a whole lot of work.

But it's not just the lost creativity, cognitive function, and productivity that take a hit when we don't stop to refuel on a regular enough basis. Willpower is annihilated and fear and anxiety run amok when you don't give your brain a chance to refuel.

In his book *How We Decide* (2009), Jonah Lehrer points to the part of the brain called the prefrontal cortex (PFC) as the seat of self-control or willpower. The problem is, the PFC is easily fatigued. In a *Wall Street Journal* article, Lehrer recounts an experiment conducted by Stanford Graduate School of Business professor Baba Shiv that divided students into two groups. While walking down a hallway, the members of one group had to recall a two-digit number, the members of the other a seven-digit number. During these walks, each student was offered a slice of chocolate cake or a bowl of fruit. The students trying to remember the seven-digit number were twice as likely to choose cake. Remembering the extra five digits so increased what Shiv called the "cognitive load" on their PFCs that their brains literally lost their ability to resist the cake.

Willpower, it turns out, is a depletable resource. Tasks that involve heavy thinking, working memory, concentration, and creativity tax the PFC in a major way, and as Shiv's experiment shows, it doesn't take all that much to draw your willpower tank down to near zero. Remembering five extra digits turns fruit into cake.

Why should you care? Two reasons. What we often experience as resistance, desire, distraction, burnout, fatigue, frustration, and anxiety in the process of creating something from nothing may, at least in part, be PFC depletion that reduces our willpower to zero and makes it near impossible to commit to the task at hand—especially if the task wars with our creative orientation. In addition, what so many creators experience as a withering ability to handle the anxiety, doubt, and uncertainty as a project nears completion may actually be self-induced rather than process-induced suffering.

Think about your own process. As you near the launch of a new venture, the completion of a manuscript, or the creation of a collection of artwork for an upcoming show, you tend to put in more hours. You work for longer periods of time without breaks. You sleep less and do so more fitfully. You stop exercising, meditating, listening to music, and creating deliberate space in your day. You eat like hell (or don't eat enough) and push away conversations and activities that take you away from your endeavor because you just don't have the time (or so you think—more on that as the chapters unfold). You abandon your more humane creation routine and rituals in the name of getting it done.

What happens? All those things stack on top of each other to systematically juice your PFC and empty your willpower tank, then keep it empty. You'll very likely experience that loss of willpower and hit to your ability to self-regulate your behavior as the evil, nasty resistance getting stronger as you get closer to completing your endeavor. In reality, a series of subtle shifts in your own behavior are causing much of the distress.

If you're someone who creates largely in a vacuum, as you get closer to the end of your endeavor you're also starting to get to the place where you've got to go public or at least reveal your creation to the first line of your potential "judges." Exposure to judgment and risk of loss begin to become far more real to you. That kicks the amygdala's fear and anxiety responses into high gear at a point when your PFC is too wiped out to do much to counter it.

Well-planned, burst-driven creation rituals with recovery periods go a long way toward taming the evil nasties that arise as a project progresses by allowing the PFC to refuel along the way. I experimented with this when writing this book. When I wrote my earlier book, *Career Renegade*, I spent the final week slumped on the couch in the tattered remains of an extra-heavy Champion sweatshirt from college—writing, sweating, thinking, muttering, spinning, and randomly cursing for the better part of sixteen hours a day. Not fun. I felt a bit like I was waging creative warfare.

This time around, I committed to a ritual that was much closer to Schwartz's. I still donned the ancient sweatshirt. And the week before the manuscript was due, I still had a ton of work to do on it. But I stuck to my bursts, took breaks to meditate, eat, play guitar, walk outside, play with my wife and daughter, and talk to friends. Amazingly enough, the work still got done, but the process became substantially more humane. Lesson learned.

PUTTING IT TOGETHER

Certainty anchors, dropped both within the context of your broader life and the boundaries of a specific creative endeavor, can be highly effective tools to counter the pull of fear, anxiety, and resistance. Those things often manifest as distraction and paralysis when you lean into uncertainty and work on the part of the process that is less intrinsically rewarding to you. While certainty anchors come in many flavors (as we'll explore later), rituals and routines are among the most common and most effective approaches. Whether you're about to start a new endeavor or are deep into your current one, take a step back and examine the following suggestions:

Explore Your Lifestyle Ritual

Look at your life outside of your primary creative endeavor and see if you can create routine around the mundane, day-to-day activities.

Identify Your Creative Orientation

Figure out which creative orientation fills you up and which empties you out: insight and big-idea generation, or refinement, expansion, and production. You may be able to evolve your starting orientation over time, but with rare exceptions we all come to the process with certain strong preferences.

Ritualize Your Creation Time and Work in Bursts and Therapeutic Pauses

When building your creation rituals, limit your bursts to no more than forty-five to ninety minutes, at least in the beginning. You may be able to train yourself to stay focused longer over time.

Refuel Your Brain Between Bursts

Between those bursts, exercise, meditate, nap, walk, eat—do whatever helps you refuel. These activities help to power up your cognitive abilities and refill your willpower tank, allowing you to stay more committed to your ritual with greater ease.

Certainty anchors help counter the potential dark side of creative uncertainty. Still, we're just beginning to build our toolbox. There is an often destructive dynamic that unfolds when we introduce exposure to judgment into the creators' journey. Judgment is impossible to fully eliminate, nor do we want to, but most people experience it as pain, so we need to develop a better understanding of its role, why it must be there, and how to effectively invite and harness it.

5

BUILD YOUR HIVE

ON A GORGEOUS summer day in Boulder, Colorado, ten teams of eager entrepreneurs and soon-to-be entrepreneurs pour into a 10,000-square-foot co-working space just off Pearl Street. Known to its inhabitants as the TechStars "bunker," it's become legend in the local community. Over the next three months, the hand-picked founding teams—generally two to five individuals seeking to launch a new business—will live and breathe nearly every waking hour and many sleeping hours here. They'll subsist on a small stipend, just enough to take care of their basic housing and day-to-day needs, guided closely by a rich community of seasoned entrepreneurs, fueled by the occasional bacon peanut butter cupcake from Tee & Cakes, around the corner. After having been accepted based on a brief online application and a live interview, many will end up radically changing not only their products, but their entire business model, sometimes many times over. Entire sites and applications will be designed, built, tested, refined, killed, redesigned, and rebuilt.

These three months will be, by all accounts, one of the most grueling, heart-breaking, inspiring, educational, transformative experiences of each participant's life.

All of this is in service of a quest—to launch a new technology-based solution and company in a massively accelerated way.

At the end of the twelfth week, TechStars will take over a local theater, where each team will present to an audience of a few hundred of the world's top angel investors and venture capitalists in the hope of landing enough funding to push their ventures through to the next level.

Of those who start the process, an astonishingly high percentage will either get funded through to the next level or generate enough revenue to bootstrap their growth from that point forward.

Either way, the environment and dynamic put in place during those twelve weeks, though utterly unsustainable over a long period of time, will have radically altered many of the fundamental aspects of the typical creation and launch process and enabled a level of success rarely experienced by entrepreneurs in the outside world.

TechStars, by the way, is not alone in its approach. The granddaddy of what's now become known as the tech "seed accelerator" model is Y Combinator, a venture started in Silicon Valley by Robert Morris; Trevor Blackwell; entrepreneur, investor, and essayist Paul Graham; and entrepreneur and author of *Founders at Work* (2007), Jessica Livingston. Every year, more than 1,000 founder teams apply for a few dozen spots. Even before investors Yuri Milner and Ron Conway offered to fund every Y Combinator start-up with $150,000 in early 2011, Graham reported a 94 percent funding rate for Y Combinator goods. Of course, getting funded or becoming bootstrap cash-flow positive isn't the same as succeeding long term. But it is a major milestone, one that the vast majority of start-ups never hit.

The seed accelerator pace, if undertaken as an ongoing endeavor, would kill even the staunchest entrepreneur. The question is what is it about this model that makes it such a powerful catalyst for radical creation, innovation, and entrepreneurship? And what elements might we be able to integrate in a creative culture that would help counter the fear of judgment, increase the tolerance for uncertainty and risk of loss, and bolster creativity on a more sustainable level?

LEVELING THE JUDGMENT PLAYING FIELD

Part of the power of the seed accelerator model lies in the energy of the hive and the expectations established around risk, uncertainty, and judgment.

Though the concepts behind each founding team arrive at varying levels of maturity (some teams have ideas; others have functioning products, platforms, and businesses), the expectation is that every person in every team still has a ton to learn. Relative to the mentors, grads, and big-name celebrity serial entrepreneurs they'll meet over the next three months, they're all newbies. They're in the same boat, living together in a frenzied state of work, ideation, execution, chaos, and constant evolution. It's a bit like Shambala Buddhism founder Chogyam Trungpa Rinpoche's famous quote: "The bad news is you're falling through the air, nothing to hang on to, no parachute. The good news is there's no ground."

When you're in the hive, there's no ground. For anyone. Every team is in a similar place relative to the long-term progression, the paths their companies are expected to travel. And that dynamic creates a certain leveling of the psychic playing field. All the founders make a presentation to the group on a weekly basis. There are no secrets. Nobody gets selective protection. Everyone is exposed. Transparency is the rule. Judge others at the risk of being judged the next time you crash and burn . . . and you will.

There's also a clear expectation set by the kindly overlords of both Y Combinator and TechStars that, regardless of the idea, product, or business model that got a team into the program, there's a good chance that some or all of it will need to be radically retooled or even completely chucked. In start-up parlance, the teams may need to "pivot" multiple times before they figure out what actually works and is worth pushing forward.

This dynamic doesn't remove judgment, nor should it. As we've already noted, judgment, done well, is feedback, and feedback is manna to the creation process. But what it does is change the psychology of feedback by leveling the field. It creates a group dynamic in which each creator becomes far more open to input because that input is clearly driven by the desire to help improve the creation. The all-in nature of the feedback loop also helps lessen the blow. It's not just your ideas that are being put on the block; everyone's ideas are. That's the process. And that's a good, necessary thing, as long as it's done right.

ALL HIVES ARE NOT CREATED EQUAL

Before I go skipping along about the merits of creative hives, it's important to note that all creative hives or community workspaces are not created equal.

Just as the right energy can create a dynamic that fosters transparency, creative risk, and a willingness to lean into uncertainty and even welcome judgment in the name of accelerated growth, the wrong energy can crush it.

We've all either heard about these environments or been ravaged by them (some of you may even have played the role of tormenter—think "teacher of newbies").

Hives have a pecking order, whether informal or established. There is always a structure and a leader, and the overall tone and emotional state of the collective experience is often set by the person or people at the top. Over time, such an emotional state can become baked into a culture and deeply affect both the moods of those who participate in the culture and what they create.

The dejected end of the emotional spectrum tends to rear its ugly head fairly often in what might be considered more traditionally creative or artistic communities, in part because those fields tend to feature creative output that has strong direct connection to emotion. Such hives are less about building a model or a functional business around the needs of people and more about the creator or the immediate community.

There's also a lot of mythology around the need to suffer, to denigrate and be denigrated as a prerequisite for the creation of great art. I don't buy into that equation, nor do I see creative communities that are defined by an exaltation of suffering and marginalizing as either personally healthy or professionally valuable. Leaning into uncertainty, risk, and judgment are mandatory. The whole point of this book, however, is to help make a whole lot of the suffering side of the equation optional.

WHAT IF YOU'RE A SOLO CREATOR?

The creative engines that TechStars co-founders David Cohen and Brad Feld and Y Combinator founders Graham, Livingston, and company have created are powerful catalysts for innovation, rapid evolution of ideas, and execution. But not every creator gets to play in the TechStars or Y Combinator playgrounds. In their most recent admissions round, Y Combinator had more than 1,000 applications for only a few dozen spots.

What do you do if you're not accepted? Or what if you're a writer, painter, dancer, or more traditionally solo-oriented creative? Is there some way to build your own creative culture and psychological scaffolding that will allow you to brave risk, exposure to judgment, and uncertainty in the quest to create on a higher level?

Absolutely. The latest incarnations of creation hives, driven by tech entrepreneurship, are just the new kids on the creative-commune block. Creators of all ilks have been finding or building their own similar communities for centuries, if not millennia.

About a year before beginning my earlier book, *Career Renegade*, an author friend of mine who was then a columnist for the *New York Times* shared how she'd been in an intimate writer's group that met in an apartment on the Upper West Side of Manhattan. Her schedule was nuts, so she had to step aside, and she asked if I wanted to step in. I said sure, not really knowing what to expect. For the better part of a year, four of us met on a monthly basis to share ideas, ask questions, share industry information, contacts, ideas for content, books, chapters, titles, designs, launch tactics, and anything else that came up. There were no stupid questions, or depending how you looked at it, there were only stupid questions, but that was okay. From those conversations came both amazing ideas and great relationships (and a number one *New York Times* best seller).

Opportunities to cultivate judgment-leveling creative hives exist in nearly every field. Yes, even if you're the solo lint sculptor in a town of 526 people. If you have an Internet connection, the communal-creative world has been flattened and woven together in ways that weren't possible even three years ago.

This opportunity is part of what fueled former Goldman Sachs banker Scott Belsky, author of *Making Ideas Happen* (2010), to launch what would rapidly grow into a network of massive online creative communities—Behance.com, Behance.net, and The99Percent.com— to be followed by the 99% Conference, an annual conference devoted to creative execution.

According to Belsky, the idea behind Behance.com was to "empower creative professionals to make ideas happen." That started with a drive to create the company's Action Method products and solutions, and quickly led Belsky and his team to create Behance.net, a place where individual artists and design professionals showcase their work, increase their visibility, and discover other creators, connecting with and learning from them. This mission was expanded upon with the launch of The99Percent.com, an online community that has grown into a remarkable professional resource, as well as a valuable source of conversation, feedback, and community. For those looking for a more hands-on experience, Belsky launched the 99% Conference, held annually in New York City.

Burgeoning sculptor Peter Wallace took a very different approach to building his creative hive. When we met, he was furiously at work in the corner office of a 10,000-square-foot loft space known as the Brooklyn Artists Gym (BAG). Wallace founded BAG in 2005 as the stepping-off point for what would become a nearly all-consuming quest for him.

After decades as a director of stage plays and movies, repeated exposure to one of history's most horrific clips of documentary film—bodies being dumped like refuse into a mass grave during the Holocaust—left him rattled to the point of needing to find or create an opposite countering image.

The solution came in a dream, as detailed and vivid as a movie: a massive wave, populated by fifty-five people of all sizes and shapes frolicking and surfing in a state of absolute bliss. A mental snapshot of the absolute peak, as the wave's crest coincided with a collective state of maximum joy, would become Wallace's "blueprint" for a life-size metal sculpture that he felt compelled to create.

Except that Peter Wallace wasn't a sculptor. He had no knowledge of how to pull off his vision, no skills, no space that could accommodate a 40-foot-wide, 20-foot-tall, 20-foot-deep metal behemoth, and nowhere near the funding to cover even the initial $300,000 it would cost just to make casts of the fifty-five people, let alone complete the work.

Speaking to Wallace was a bit like sitting across the kitchen from Kevin Costner's character in the movie *Field of Dreams*. He didn't know how it would happen; he just knew the piece had to be built. Indeed, he even knew the exact hill in San Francisco where the massive sculpture should sit. Step one was finding a space to make it happen and a community of artisans to learn from and work with. The size of the space he needed so far exceeded his budget that he realized he would need to take a radical approach.

With that, the idea for Brooklyn Artists Gym, a shared artist's creative-hive space in Brooklyn, was born. Artists of all types rent space in exchange for a monthly membership fee. Some of the space is allocated as assigned creative zones, but in a larger space, reserved for open creation, artists show up, pull their current creations from storage racks, set up, create, clean up, and leave.

I was fascinated by the social dynamic of the community Wallace was building. In addition to devoted artists, there were absolute newbies and those returning to their passion after years away. Media ranged from sculpture to massive oil canvases to illustration; there were artists as young as twenty and as old as eighty. A smaller private room ("Room 58") was set aside for writers, and yet another room off that one, was for journalists, who could make phone calls as necessary.

I wondered how the diversity of experience, age, ability, and medium affected the social dynamic in the space. Wallace said that while many of the artists become inspired by those a bit more accomplished than they are, some of the artists also feel too exposed. What they really want, he said, is a tiny nest where no one can see them. They want an incubation process, but they don't like to be watched. So BAG doesn't end up working for them. On the other end of the spec-

trum, there are those who arrive a bit daunted and then blossom because of the exposure and the potential for judgment.

"The nature of this space," Wallace said, "is you have to be okay
with it, sort of like the notion that you may be working around artists
whom you perceive as further down the road from you . . . and knowing that they are going to see what you're doing and taking that as an
opportunity rather than oppression."

Wallace's comment highlights the importance, for solo artists looking to join a hive, of understanding the currents and ethics that fuel
the particular community:

- Is it cutthroat and competitive?
- Is it laid-back and collaborative?
- Is it social or segregated?
- Is it more about relationship building or getting work done?
- Are the creators who populate it productive?
- Is it cooperative, or is it pay to play, with no sense of service to
  the community?
- Will it leave you feeling pushed yet supported, or exposed and
  defeated?
- Is it more about judgment leveling or feeling judged and leveled?

Before committing to any hive, you need to do your research and
tap into its creative zeitgeist. Otherwise you may discover that the
experience you'd hoped would bolster your efforts ends up crushing
them instead. Which, in the end, is also one of the biggest arguments
in favor of doing what Wallace did and creating his own from the
ground up.

If you can't do it live, do it online. We saw an example of that in
Scott Belsky's creation of Behance.net and The99Percent.com. These
are both huge creative communities catering to the broader set of

"creatives who like to get stuff done." Now, with millions of monthly page views, they serve as tremendous showcases and sources of feedback for the participants' work. For Belsky, the communities also serve as gateways to the suite of wonderful creative productivity tools under his Action Method brand.

But what if you're just one person with a much more specific interest in finding a group of people to trade ideas with and who will offer support around your passion or craft? This is exactly the position Adam King, a furniture maker and woodworker based in Olney, Illinois, found himself in at the start of 2010.

After years of slipping in and out of depression and struggling with both his craft and his career—a phenomenon that's sadly not all that foreign to many a solo creator—King turned to the Internet as a way to connect with people and potentially find like-minded, supportive friends and woodworkers. What he discovered and then built exceeded his every expectation.

He began to play around on Twitter, joining in conversations with woodworkers and unconventional entrepreneurs all over the world. Finding commonality, King began to build friendships and realized how the sense of community was changing him and bringing him back to both the world and his work.

In the second half of the year, he took things to a new level after stumbling upon a relatively untapped twist on the Twitter experience—Twitter chats, ongoing public conversations led by a chat facilitator around a designated topic. Anyone can start a Twitter chat. Chat leaders announce a date and time for a chat to begin, along with the topic and a hashtag (a short snippet of text that starts with #, followed by the name of the chat). At the designated date and time, the leader begins the conversation, often with a question as an opening prompt; followers reply and add to conversation through 140-character "tweets" punctuated by the relevant hashtag. You can attach links to images, URLs, or pretty much any additional media you'd like to bring to the chat. The entire conversation can be followed in real time and participated by following the hashtag. Many people use external client Web sites that update a designated hashtag in real time, then let you add your voice.

King wondered if he could assemble a worldwide creative community that would share ideas and insights on woodworking and support one another through the vehicle of a weekly Twitter chat. With that, #woodchat, a weekly Twitter chat on all things wood, came to life. "Into 2011," King told me, "#woodchat has become the main source for me in regard to listening. It's the only time that the collective comes together and openly discusses exactly what they're having difficulties with and what solutions would serve them best. Talk about a gold mine! Not to mention it's now in a position to be sponsored on a regular basis by woodworking tool companies, magazines, and other related services that have recently come online."

How might King take his hive to the next level? He could consider moving some of the conversation to a private forum, where the "closed doors" would provide enough protection from judgment by random digital "trolls" for the artists to expose even more about themselves, their work, and their journeys. He could incorporate weekly "digital dinners," the way Paul Graham and his team do live with their Y Combinator founders, where all participants could reveal what they've created and benefit from "benevolent" judgment and constructive insight. He could bring in mentors—vetting them, of course, to ensure they are there to help all participants prosper. All of which, it turns out, is exactly what King has already built the beginnings of with WoodWorkersJourney.com.

Until now, we've focused largely on the role of changing the dynamic of creation-critical judgment from colleagues and peers in an effort to benefit from the data they provide while minimizing the suffering side of the experience. But there's another major source of potential constructive judgment that's often the most terrifying, yet helpful source of growth available: accomplished people in your field. It is also one of the driving forces behind the success of hive-driven programs like Y Combinator and TechStars.

MENTORS, HEROES, AND CHAMPIONS

Since launching in 2007, TechStars has expanded its program to a number of locations. But each location runs the program only once a year. When I asked TechStars co-founder Brad Feld why they don't just keep pushing new teams through every three months, he said there were two equally important limitations.

First, he and his co-founder, David Cohen, have limited bandwidth. They're both accomplished, involved entrepreneurs and investors outside of TechStars, and both have families and rich personal lives. When TechStars is in session, it requires an immense investment of their time and energy in all aspects, from mentoring to administration to building and expanding the TechStars brand into a worldwide presence.

Second, beyond benefiting from the collective energy and emphasis on experimentation and pivot, the founding teams have access not only to Feld and Cohen, but to a sizable family of highly accomplished local business mentors. The teams are strongly encouraged to meet with these mentors as often as possible and to build real relationships with them. The sense of confidence these interactions instill goes a long way toward reinforcing the ability to lean into fear and uncertainty because the mentors have been there, done that, struggled and suffered, and lived to tell about it, often many times over. They serve as mission-critical sources of information and insight—and proof that no matter how uncertain the quest, success is possible.

Reece Pacheco, a co-founder of Shelby.TV and a participant in the inaugural 2011 New York TechStars program, points to his mentoring team as having been mission critical in the start-up's ability to relentlessly evolve and adapt to what the mentors believed the market most needed. Having access to seasoned tech investors and entrepreneurship experts—like Fred Wilson of Union Square Ventures, Flatiron Partners' Jerry Collona, Karin Klein at the Bloomberg First Growth Venture Network, Mike Duda at Consigliere, and Rachel Sklaar of Hashable—enabled them to do what would have been near impossible in a vacuum. The mentors helped the founding team come up with ideas, plan, build, pivot, and launch, sometimes a few times over in a highly compressed time frame. Besides adding information and insight, they changed the psychology of creation in a substantial way, pulling the founding team perpetually out onto uncertain ground in the name of challenging perceived limitations and making something better.

The mentors also work to move their creative protégés to a place where their creations, mind-sets, and abilities are developed enough so that by the time the founding teams graduate and the mentors pull back to reclaim a bit more normalcy, the founders are far better equipped to continue moving forward, though likely not at the same pace.

Like Feld and Cohen, these mentors lead incredibly busy lives, often running companies, serving on the boards of others, consulting and investing actively. Though many remain in close contact with the founding teams they connect most closely with, they too lack the bandwidth to continue to invest so heavily beyond the hyperfocused twelve-week window.

Mentoring can play an extraordinary role in cultivating the mind-set needed to take creative risks and keep operating in that anxious place where the best stuff tends to be birthed—especially when your mentor is someone who's been where you are, lived, breathed, and danced with the same or similar-enough demons and elations, and found a way to harness them to create genius. This experience of walking in a mentee's shoes helps a mentor not only sympathize but empathize and draw upon the appropriate insights gained.

Mentoring, of course, is not exclusive to high-tech seed accelerators. In 2008 Ishita Gupta met Seth Godin, an entrepreneur and marketing thought leader. She would eventually come to work with Godin, first as a student in his alternative MBA program and later as a full-time employee. Gupta also sees Godin as an influential mentor. Under his guidance, Gupta launched an online magazine called fear. less (fearlessstories.com).

Working with Godin, she told me, "pushes you to be at the top of your game. It forces you to recognize that a level of success is there and can be attainable and is up for grabs." She admits that the experience has been intimidating at times. But in the end, the realization that "wow, this person believes in me" has empowered her to do things she might not have otherwise thought possible.

Beyond direct insight and guidance, mentoring also serves a secondary, mind-set-driven role. It is direct proof that the quest to create something that's never been done before can pay dividends. It may not be easy, but there is a potential light at the end of the tunnel— sometimes even a raging inferno.

Godin himself acknowledges the power of mentors, but he also thinks they're vastly overrated. "If you are lucky enough to have somebody who will pay a lot of attention to what you're doing, then great, more power to you," he told me. "But the search for their magic . . . I'm just not buying it." He fears that people are tempted to use a failure to find a good mentor as an excuse; he rejects the idea that "you can't be creative because you don't have a mentor, and if only that guy would stop being so selfish and tell you what to do, you'd be fine."

Instead Godin recommends that we seek out heroes, accomplished individuals who can inspire us by example without having to provide individual feedback and support. While mentors can be powerful allies and catalysts, a substantial chunk of what they offer can be provided by finding and studying the right heroes. For many, heroes will be far easier to find than mentors, and the lack of a mentor should never be pointed to as the reason for your own lack of will, action, or progress.

In addition to the mentor and the hero, there's one other potential member of the creation-support team who can shift the psychology of the quest in a profound way—the champion.

Remember Erik Proulx, the laid-off ad man who became a documentary filmmaker? As Proulx explored a variety of his own creative endeavors, he kept reaching out to friends to partner with. But, every one said, "That sounds amazing, but my spouse/partner said no, so I can't do it." Had Proulx's wife turned to him and said, "You need to get a job, pronto," the dream would have ended. He would have honored her request. But she didn't say that. Somehow she too knew he had to make the movie. It wasn't just his quest; it was their quest. That faith, Proulx shared with me, may have been the greatest gift of love, belief, and confidence he's ever been given.

When *Lemonade* failed to make it into the big festivals and get the distribution and funding he'd hoped for, Proulx was forced to revisit the justification for his quest. When he thought he'd have to give up his house to make his vision happen, his wife was on board. And when he figured out how to craft a new blended path that honored both his need to tell stories on film and his desire to get paid to do similar things for commercial clients, his wife said, "Go for it."

I've never talked with Proulx about what his wife's support has meant to him without his being on the verge of tears. That gift was stunning. It enabled his to act on a dream. It transformed *his* quest into *their* quest and not only made his creation journey possible, but altered the uncertainty and judgment dynamic in a way that allowed him to take risks and create on a level that would have been impossible had he been locked in a battle for support.

Proulx's wife had become his champion, someone deeply invested in his journey and equally devoted to seeing its manifestation. Fans, those who watch from the side and cheer you on, come and go. Champions are more difficult to find. They are people who will be there with you, no matter what happens, especially ones who will feel the pain equally, both emotionally and financially, if you fail. Armed with their confidence, any person who is embarked on a creation quest becomes empowered on a very different level. The psychology changes. The champion's confidence in you fortifies you against the destructive judgment that can come from both without and within; it allows you the latitude to create edgier, riskier, more button-pushing work.

I know this through the story of Proulx and so many others, as well as through my own experience with my wife. We've both been involved in the world of entrepreneurship for many years. And we've both left behind high-earning careers that required years of study, accreditation, prestige, and at least the perception of security. When, shortly before we married, I told her of my desire to leave a six-figure income as a lawyer to make $12 an hour as a personal trainer, she could have flipped out. She could have fought me. But she didn't. She knew that, at the time, it was the thing that I couldn't not do.

She believed that if I could succeed in a world in which I had little interest, I'd figure out a way to succeed again in a world whose light pulled me in, even if most others failed. That trust, that faith, that commitment has been the bedrock of my ability to do much of what I have done professionally since that moment. It's helped me launch numerous other companies and endeavors and change careers and gears. It kept me sane when, eight weeks after 9/11, with a three-month-old baby in tow, I launched a yoga center in the heart of New York City while businesses all around us were crashing. My wife is my champion, and I am hers. And I cannot tell you how profoundly that knowledge has changed my ability to create, innovate, build, and take the risks that have brought me to this place in life.

PUTTING IT TOGETHER

The goal of any creative hive is to create a dynamic in which the following five qualities define the experience:

Groups of People, Teams or Individuals, Are Questing on a Similar Level

This doesn't mean everyone you work with needs to be equally skilled or talented or at the same level of success, income, or fame. Rather, your hive should share a common openness to the notion that they're all there to learn, to make mistakes, and to share and invite a high degree of feedback.

Transparency Is Heightened

Some communities go so far as to adopt a radical transparency philosophy, meaning everything is laid bare and nothing is kept private. I haven't often seen that level of exposure work, at least not outside the realm of group therapy, which is what it often devolves into. But what you want to do is create the expectation that on a daily basis everyone will be fairly exposed to the processes and output of others, and that on a weekly basis there will be a period of "kindly reckoning." All persons or teams will present their work, explain what's brought them to where they are, then step back and be open to the input of others, both peers and mentors.

Nobody is protected in the weekly "reveal," which helps cultivate a good mix of kindness and honesty. You know your head's on the block next. Even if this week was good, there'll be bad ones. There always are. And it's nice to be able to receive input on those weeks in a frame that empowers rather than crushes you.

It's a Zillion-Sum Game

One person's success isn't necessarily another person's loss. There is no zero-sum game. It must be assumed that all ships can rise, and the more that rise, the better it is for everyone. It's not about how you'll carve up an existing pie or grab money or attention from other creators in the hive; it's about how you'll rally together to expand the existing pie to make room for all and maybe even bake a few new flavors.

John T. Unger, an artist and metalworker who creates artisanal fire-bowl sculptures that are outdoor, welded, bowl-shaped fire enclosures made from recycled metals, calls this the "zillion-sum game":

> It's like I need to win but the customer should win, but ideally so should my employees and vendors and the innocent bystanders. If somebody buys a Firebowl, they're happy they got art; I'm happy I got paid. The freight company is happy 'cause they got to ship something. But also everybody that comes over to the house for dinner and sits around the fire is happy.
>
> . . . and artists are happy because there's somebody out there proving you can make a living and showing them how to do it. And it's like ideally, I try really hard to make sure that I don't ever do things that are just selfishly for my own benefit. Somebody else should get something out of it too.

Whether you join a hive or build your own, that's the energy you're looking for: like that of the artists embracing Unger's zillion-sum game.

There Is a Demonstrated Commitment to a Culture That Embraces Experimentation

Trial, error, and recovery should be exalted. Doing what nobody's done before you and failing in a wild public fashion is not a badge of honor, but the will to push the envelope boldly and consistently is seen as a virtue. Nobody is looking to kick the next person or team off the island. It's all about fostering the ability for every team to stay on the island long enough to build their own islands.

When you create an environment with all five elements, you strip away a lot of the fear of judgment and intolerance for uncertainty that stifles creativity and innovation. Those who would normally judge you at your level are encouraged to keep their comments constructive, rather than destructive, because they're all exposed. Those in a position to judge from above have been where you are and are invested in having you repeatedly try and fail in the name of discovering what works.

The goal of the judgment-leveling hive is not a Darwinian survival of the fittest, but rather an elevation of everyone. It's not a zero-sum creative game. While judgment or feedback in this context might not be "fun," there's an understanding that it's being offered not in the name of tearing down, shunning, or disqualifying anyone, but rather as a source of guidance for the next big experiment.

Former head of education for Pixar, Randy Nelson, put it beautifully when he said, "The core skill of innovators is not failure avoidance, it's error recovery." When that's baked into your creative culture on all levels, people become more empowered to lean into the creative abyss—and magic tends to happen.

Creators Have Access to Mentors, Heroes, and Champions

As we've seen, mentors, heroes, and champions can be extraordinary allies in the quest to bring something new to life. In the context of a hive, either build or find a culture that helps you build relationships with mentors and champions. They can provide knowledge, insights, feedback, support, and, as needed, swift kicks in the ass. Places like TechStars and Y Combinator publicize their mentors in advance, and access to these people is often one of the deciding factors for entrepreneurs applying to any particular program.

It's the same thing if you're a solo creator. Your hive might be people you already know or people one or two degrees of connection away. Look at the people in your industry or field whose work, lifestyle, and accomplishments you admire and whom you'd most like to learn from. If you have someone who can make an introduction, that is generally the best option. I've found that with many extraordinary creators now setting up camp across social media, it's now easier than ever to find these people, participate in the communities they're creating, and build genuine relationships that, over time, can have the potential to evolve into more of a mentoring experience.

Taking classes with people you'd like to eventually develop a mentoring relationship with or becoming involved in organizations they're involved in are also possible options to explore. However, do not take a class, become involved in a community, or join an organization purely because you want something from someone. You should have a genuine interest in the broader mission and experience of the group or community. The opportunity to connect with another member with whom you'd like to build a relationship will then come much more organically. Believe it or not, it is possible to stalk and spam people not just online, but in person. Don't do that.

So far, we've explored how making certain changes in behavior (certainty anchors, ritual, routine, working in bursts), environment (hives), and access to individuals (like-minded colleagues, mentors, heroes, and champions) can have a significant impact on your ability to lean into the uncertainty, exposure to judgment, and risk that come with the process of creation. A bit later, we'll dive deep into a set of daily personal practices that can profoundly humanize and energize the process.

Before we go there, what if there was a way to alter the process that inspires relentless action, fundamentally changes the uncertainty dynamic from day one, and preserves your ability to bring to life extraordinary outcomes? Would you want in?

That's where we're going in the next chapter.

6

SOCIALIZING CREATION

WELL-CRAFTED, CONSTRUCTIVE CREATION hives, buttressed by peer feedback and guidance from mentors, heroes, and champions, can be powerful supports in the quest to embrace the uncertainty of creation. They allow us to get the information we need to move the creative ball forward while minimizing the anxiety that often comes from haphazard exposure to less tactful or even maliciously inclined colleagues and leaders. But there's something else that's begun to emerge over the last few years that may well signal a far more radical change in the process of creation and in the deeper psychology that underlies it. This change, applicable across a wide variety of fields, is being led through the vehicle of technology.

A huge part of the uncertainty, fear, and anxiety that defines the typical quest to create comes from a lack of input during the process of creation from those we'd most like to appeal to with our creations. When we plan a business, book, painting, or product, we take our best guesses at what will work. Then we work to either find the sweet spot between what we are organically compelled to create and what we believe people will want or ignore those we hope will eventually love our creations in the name of staying true to our muse. The process, for many, is largely blind. And that often leads to extraordinary levels of uncertainty, fear, anxiety, and suffering.

Some industries try to add the appearance of input from the ultimate consumer in the form of focus groups, data mining, or customer questionnaires. These are often riddled with bias or influenced by payment and the desire to please the marketers. At times, these "market research" tools are really just cover-your-ass vehicles. They give the creators something tangible to point to as proof they weren't nuts after an endeavor bombs.

Others, generally on the traditional artist side of the creative spectrum, shun the very idea of considering the preferences, insights, or input of those whose approval, enjoyment, and money they'll eventually seek, claiming any such involvement would not only taint but outright bastardize the process. What people think of you and your creation, they say, is none of your business.

That is an easy enough stance to adopt, but if you plan on trying to earn a living selling what you create, it can be a pretty brutal position to maintain, both financially and psychologically. The claim of creative purity is often invoked as a crutch to avoid having to rise to a number of challenges:

- Creating on a level that builds powerful enough experiences to matter in the lives of others.
- Learning how to effectively market your work without feeling you've lost your soul.
- Having your peers call you a sellout when your financial success makes them uncomfortable about their own unwillingness to create great art that pays the rent.

What if there was a way to bring the very people you are creating for (other than yourself) into the process *while* you're creating, to learn what works in microbits along the way, providing you with enough insight about your creation on a regular basis to give you substantially more certainty about the desirability of each creative fragment? What if you could do it without diluting your vision? It would make the process of creation so much more confident, humane, and likely to succeed, by nearly any definition of the word.

In the last few years, advances in technology have made this kind of iterative feedback possible on a level that makes a real difference. This approach offers the potential to create better solutions more quickly, with less waste, greater impact, far less suffering, and in the case of entrepreneurship, far less financial cost.

DARREN ROWSE: IF THEY DIG IT, I WILL BUILD IT

Working from cafés in a suburb outside of Melbourne, Australia, Darren Rowse has become a bit of a legend in the blogosphere. Over the last seven years, he's built two of the world's leading niche content properties—Problogger (problogger.net), the premier destination for information on making money blogging, and Digital Photography School (DPS), one of the largest online photography educational sites. Both contribute tremendous value to their readers, and both generate a substantial profit.

When Rowse started, the blogosphere wasn't what it is today. The thought of adding the element of commerciality to a blog was considered heresy by many, a total bastardization of what blogs were about: the free exchange of information and conversation.

The blogosphere can be a brutal place to be an envelope pusher. With the advent of comments and the cost of starting your own blog now rounding to zero, everyone has a voice. If you piss people off, you know it. If you tread on sacred ground, you're likely to be publicly excoriated. If you violate the unwritten rules and ethics or ask more of your readers than they're ready to give, they'll let you know.

But there's a glorious flip side to this dynamic. Blogs also provide the opportunity for those you most want to serve and delight to tell you when you're on the right track and, if not, how they'd like you to get there. That capability became a core tool in Rowse's creation arsenal. Every time he'd experiment with a new feature, topic, design element, or attempt at monetization, he'd keep a very close eye on the comments section of the blogs. It wasn't unusual for him to know, within minutes, whether his latest evolution was a hit, a dud, or somewhere in the middle. Rowse came to rely heavily on this cycle of constant evolution and feedback in his quest to create the best possible solution and, eventually, business. "My philosophy," Rowse told me, "has always been just to start it and then again just start testing to see whether it's worth spending any money on it . . . I've always been very conservative on that front . . . I don't like to start things that I don't think will work, and I don't like to start things that other people don't think will work."

The opportunity to leverage the technology to constantly test new options and content, have feedback immediately pushed to him, then respond to that feedback to create something more valuable was critical in Rowse's ability to create what he's created. It guided both the content he offered and the way he developed his business model around that content. It also dramatically altered the fear and uncertainty dynamic by breaking down each forward step into small pieces. As Rowse kept building on his most recent success, he could be fairly confident his next step wouldn't incur too much wrath, even if it missed the mark.

Over time, the repeated exposure to user feedback served to diminish Rowse's potential fear of judgment and intolerance for uncertainty. The same can happen for you: The repeated exposure to criticism becomes the functional equivalent of exposure therapy, one of the core tools in the fear arsenal of cognitive behavioral therapists. The more you act in the face of it and survive, the less you feel its stranglehold. This dynamic serves as a huge confidence booster and anxiety reducer in the quest to create something from nothing.

Rowse's reliance on real-time user feedback became a critical part of his creative process. When he partnered with Chris Garrett to write a Problogger book, the far more cloistered process caused him a world of angst. "I hated it," he told me. "I wasn't getting feedback along the way, and I needed that affirmation that I was doing it correctly. I needed the comments on the posts that said yes, this is right or this is wrong."

The direct user feedback Rowse relied upon to build his company was facilitated by the technology of blogging and social media. But what about other creative endeavors? What if you're an entrepreneur relying on technology, a business model, or a creative process that doesn't allow the level of customer interaction that exists in the world of blogging and social media? What if you're a solo creator—a traditional artist, writer, dancer, or painter? Is there some way you can still access and benefit from this type of incremental prototyping, testing, learning, and user involvement?

Even if you can, should you? Or does bringing so many other voices into a more traditional artistic creative process dilute the quality and impact of the final creation, making you more likely to end up producing homogenized dreck?

GETTING LEAN

Enter "lean start-up methodology" (LSM). As the former Chief Technology Officer at IMVU, a graphical social network, LSM creator

Eric Ries became fascinated with a manufacturing process that grew out of Toyota's mass-production lines. Lean manufacturing, as it was called, focused on optimizing learning and minimizing waste. It was one of the driving forces behind the post–World War II Japanese automakers' ability to quickly compete with, then triumph over U.S.-based automakers. Ries, however, saw a way to repurpose the lean approach to the much more frenetic world of entrepreneurship and, in the process, not only accelerate progress but alter the uncertainty and fear dynamic in a substantial way.

The tenets of lean manufacturing are generally agreed to include:

1. Eliminate waste.
2. Amplify learning.
3. Decide as late as possible.
4. Deliver as fast as possible.
5. Empower the team.
6. Build in integrity.
7. See the whole.

As the co-founder and CTO at IMVU in 2004, Ries began to wonder if there was a better way to build products as well as businesses. The traditional business start-up process, he found, was littered with waste and angst. It included a laundry list of assumptions and outright leaps of faith, a tremendous amount of risk, and a lot of internal product development and business modeling based not on real data but on "educated" guesses that turned out to be anything but. Customer involvement in the building process, beyond focus groups that often yielded insights that were so skewed as to be deemed worthless, was rare.

Beyond creating a dynamic that fostered high levels of fear and uncertainty, the lack of customer involvement also created a huge amount of waste. You wouldn't know if you'd hit the mark until you had spent a lot of time, money, and energy getting your solution ready to go public. If you missed the mark, you either folded up shop or worked like crazy to retool and get it right before you ran out of runway.

This is a brutal way to launch a business, emotionally and financially. I know. I've done it. Twice. Back when I still had hair.

Ries, a hardcore technologist and entrepreneur fueled by a growing fascination with lean methodology, wondered what might happen if you tailored the lean approach not to mass production, but to one of the most creative and risky processes on the planet: launching a business.

Doing so requires a fundamental shift in focus. In the lean start-up, everything is done in the name not of profits but of learning. Teams build what Ries calls a minimum viable product (MVP) that represents the "least amount of work necessary to start learning." This product is then released to potential users as a series of experiments; feedback is solicited, then folded into the next MVP.

This methodology, detailed in Ries's book *The Lean Startup* (2011), speaks to a potential revolution in the way businesses are conceived, launched, and built—not just because it focuses on learning, rapid prototyping, customer involvement, improvement, and iteration, but because it radically alters the uncertainty, risk, and judgment dynamic of the typical start-up.

It takes the anxiety-provoking leaps of faith, assumptions, and actions that are traditionally performed in private and opens them up to the end users early and often. It takes the focus on secrecy, effort, expense, and waste built upon best guesses about who the customers are and what they'll want and shifts it to rapid, exposed, public learning, customer engagement, and feedback. It breaks down the big questions that terrify and often paralyze creators into small pieces, then injects solid-enough answers from likely users in short-enough intervals to effectively disarm fear and uncertainty.

Edward Boches, Chief Innovation Officer at the Boston-based ad firm Mullen, has been experimenting with similar innovations in the world of advertising and communications. Representing some of the largest companies in the world entails a mountain of pressure, especially in a world where you're only as good as your last campaign. Applying a modified lean approach to campaign creation is beginning to radically change both the traditional process and its underlying psychology.

In the not-too-distant past, Mullen teams conceptualized and built campaigns largely in a closed environment. A group of creatives would generate ideas, then apply a set of internal quality, taste, and judgment filters, maybe expose them to a slice of consumers, produce what they thought would work, and then put it into the marketplace.

"At the end of the day, after all the testing that we've done," Boches told me, "we still have this level of uncertainty because we have never put it into the real world. We don't actually know, despite what happens in focus groups or testing environments, whether or not it's going to be effective and also whether the rest of the world is going to think it's creative. We have spent 90 percent of our time creating something that we hope will be effective and then we spend the last 2 or 3 percent of the time sticking it into the marketplace and praying."

Advertising and marketing have evolved from blast and pray to build and engage, and Boches has jumped on the opportunity to engage in that changed dynamic in a serious way. Rather than creating in a vacuum, launching, and praying, Mullen is now building platforms, apps, and experiences that involve the potential user of the experience from the beginning; the creators are in a constant state of creation. Boches added, "I've moved through any uncertainty I've had by actually involving not just peers and colleagues whose opinions I might respect but customers and the people who are going to actually use something."

You're much less likely to remain petrified about whether your endeavor is good enough when the people in the position to answer those questions, your customers and colleagues, have been telling you whether you're on track from the get-go.

LEARNING TO PIVOT

The word "pivot," which in start-up circles means the process of making serious changes to nearly every assumption your big business idea was based on and everything that's grown out of that idea, has become one of the most tossed-around terms in the world of entrepreneurship—especially tech entrepreneurship—over the last few years.

As the legendary Silicon Valley serial entrepreneur and venture capitalist Randy Komisar revealed in his book *Getting to Plan B* (2009), the vast majority of companies, even vetted ones backed by venture capital, get serious elements of their business model, solution, and market demand completely wrong. Many of the companies Komisar's firm backed were forced to restart, some even three times, even after being funded.

A willingness and ability to own those mistakes as early and as often as possible has become exalted by a growing number of mentors, founders, and investors like Komisar as a fundamental quality of the successful entrepreneur. When you look back at the experience of the founding teams who endured the intensive twelve-week seed-accelerator energy of TechStars or Y Combinator, one of the most powerful expectations set in that environment is that regardless of what got them into the program, each team will very likely have to pivot. Founders are accepted, they're told, much more on the basis of the perceived ability of the founding team to figure out the right model and the best solution rather than the idea that the business they're walking in with is the one they'll walk out with.

Airbnb.com is a great example. Started in 2008 by a budget directory and booking service to rent air mattresses on people's floors, the founding team was having trouble getting traction. Y Combinator's Paul Graham, however, saw the team's potential and invited them into the program in January 2009. They emerged with a model that had pivoted to a short-term space rental community, boasting everything from rooms to castles and boats and a new design. With the change in model, sales began to take off. As of January 2011, according to Crunchbase.com, Airbnb.com boasted 50,000 unique listings in more than 8,000 cities and 167 countries.

The seed-accelerator model is a perfect example of what happens when you push people from big idea through rapid prototyping, customer involvement, and pivot. The iteration is driven not by the fastest path to revenue, but rather the fastest path to learning. This expression of learning has been taken almost to the level of the absurd with programs like Lean Startup Machine. In that program teams of entrepreneurs and techies show up and literally conceive, prototype, launch, solicit customer feedback, iterate, and often pivot multiple times in the quest to create something brilliant from nothing . . . in one weekend. A few years ago, this would have been impossible, but technology now makes this feat still excruciating, but doable.

When Ben Kaufman launched his next-generation online invention, the crowd-sourcing platform Quirky.com, he tapped this very dynamic as a way to add certainty to the process of choosing, building, and marketing new inventions. In high school, inspired by an idea for an iPod accessory, Kaufman convinced his folks to remortgage their house to come up with the $185,000 needed to turn the notion into a reality. With that, he launched his company, Mophie, and was off to China to find a manufacturer. That first product was a hit, and it led to a number of follow-up accessories.

When the annual MacWorld show came around and found him out of ideas for his next big product, Kaufman did something brazen. He banged together a booth of two-by-fours and invited the attendees to share ideas for things they'd like to see created in exchange for the promise that he and the community would select one, then manufacture and bring it to market—in seventy-two hours.

Kaufman was so inspired by the process that he decided to sell Mophie and launch a new company, Quirky.com, that brought together potential end users and other creators with inventors to source, refine, and manufacture new inventions. Quirky is an online platform that allows any creator or inventor to submit an idea for a product, which is then voted on, rated, and curated by a large community of participants and potential buyers. If it makes the grade, the invention passes through a number of other checkpoints, then twice a week Quirky chooses two products and actually manufactures and releases them into the market.

Prospective inventors get to minimize the risk and anxiety normally associated with developing an idea in isolation and attempting to bring it to market. Once they go public with their idea, it moves toward investment and production only when a large community of potential buyers and co-creators gives it a thumbs-up. Often, that same community helps refine and improve the invention along the way. Then Quirky takes on the financial burden of additional R&D, manufacturing, distribution, and marketing. The company manages its own risk by leaning on the insights and approval of the community.

While Kaufman's platform lacks the MVP "rapid prototyping and iteration" aspect of the lean process, his transparency and desire to bring potential users into the selection and creation process changes the uncertainty dynamic in a profound way and has inspired the manufacture and release of countless new products, while minimizing risk, fear, and suffering on the part of both Quirky and the inventors.

Creators of all types are tapping a very different online platform—Kickstarter.com—to fund their creations, solicit feedback, and even pre-sell their creations while they're still in the idea stage, altering the fear and certainty dynamic in a profound way.

According to the description on the company's Web site, Kickstarter.com is "the largest funding platform for creative projects in the world. Every month, tens of thousands of amazing people pledge millions of dollars to projects from the worlds of music, film, art, technology, design, food, publishing and other creative fields. . . . This is not about investment or lending. Project creators keep 100% ownership and control over their work."

Anyone can post an idea for a creative project on Kickstarter.com, along with details, briefs, videos, or any other content that might help persuade "digital patrons" to donate to see their creations brought to life. Projects have included books, movies, paintings, trips, and nearly any other creative endeavor you might imagine. The platform serves as a source of funding, as well as an exchange of ideas and insights about proposed projects, through creator updates and contributor comments.

It's a fairly revolutionary way to fund a creative project. Getting both feedback and non-equity-stakeholder funding changes the psychology of creation. As we've seen with Eric Ries's lean methodology, getting feedback from potential users early and often goes a long way toward quelling the fear of creating something nobody else will appreciate. Passing the funding threshold also tells you that hundreds, sometimes thousands of people believe both in you and in the vision of what you seek to create.

Just as with Quirky.com, aspiring creators still need to find the courage to "out" their ideas on Kickstarter.com. No doubt, that invokes fear of judgment and uncertainty. But it does so on the basis of a nugget of an idea before the work's begun, rather than on the basis of the final creation, which could easily have been months or years and much soul, sweat, and money in the making. The exposure happens far earlier in the process when there's a lot less on the line and it's far easier to learn from and, if desired, correct course and try again.

Certain very savvy creators have leveraged the Kickstarter process to manage uncertainty on a much larger scale, by using it as a source of insight and an indication of acceptance, and as a tool to pre-sell and manage opening inventory for creative, innovative products and businesses. There's likely no better example of this than the TikTok+LunaTik Multi-Touch Watch Kits project posted in 2010 by designer Scott Wilson and his team at Chicago-based MINIMAL design studio.

TikTok and LunaTik were intended to be sleek, industrial-designed kits that allowed iPod nano owners to transform their nanos into watches. Wilson wanted to bring these kits to life as an in-house design project, so he turned to Kickstarter as a way of testing interest, getting feedback, and raising money by promising backers different combinations and versions of the kits, pegging the pledge amounts at a fraction of what each kit or bundle would eventually cost at retail.

Wilson set his funding threshold at $15,000. One month later, the funding window ended with 13,512 backers and $941,718 in the bank. Wilson's biggest challenge was figuring out how to satisfy the insane overdemand for the product he wanted to create. During that same window, the community shared 1,476 comments on the project, and Wilson updated and responded 29 times. Think about how this process not only launched a product, but changed the psychology of fear and uncertainty attached to bringing Wilson's creation to life.

Still, the very idea of letting your ultimate user help determine your final output raises a host of questions, especially when you extend this model to solo artists in more traditional creative fields.

THE CO-CREATION ARTIST MACHINE

When Gretchen Rubin wrote her number one *New York Times* best seller *The Happiness Project* (2009), she did what she'd done in her previous books: conduct extensive research and draw upon the intellect and writing skills that started her career, years earlier, as a clerk at the United States Supreme Court. Then she veered off course a bit. In the three years preceding the book's publication, Rubin had taken to blogging and had built a substantial, engaged community. She tapped that community on a regular basis to ask questions, share ideas, and offer hints of what was coming in the book. The blog also became fertile ground to test content and see what people were responding to.

Then she went a step further and created what she called her tribe of Happiness Project "superfans," a gathering of readers who got more access to Rubin, along with the opportunity to learn more about the book and share insights and ideas. From the years-long interaction with her digital tribes, Rubin not only learned enough to help guide her own exploration of happiness, she was also able to integrate the insights and stories shared by her blog tribe into the book.

Blogger and entrepreneurship coach Pam Slim did something similar with her book *Escape from Cubicle Nation* (2009), creating a subtribe, then reaching out to them about ideas and topics for the book and sharing bits of her process here and there.

I often tap my own blog, Twitter, and Facebook communities to test ideas and potential writing topics. Having seen how effective Rubin's and Slim's tribes were in helping craft and then market their books, during the late stages of writing this book I created my own digital "creation tribe." I offered to share increased access to my thoughts, writing and publication process, and ideas in exchange for their occasional insights and input on various things while I wrote. My goal was to involve them in my process, and also to make sure I honored everyone's participation by giving as much, if not more, than I was getting. I conducted a number of private educational conference calls with them, since many were authors and aspiring authors too, and shared insights on the process that most people aren't exposed to.

Engaging your readers in an ongoing conversation is one way to tap technology to obtain greater confidence that you'll create something people will enjoy. But what about going back and rewriting an already published work based on the feedback of readers?

That's exactly what Joely Black, an epic fantasy writer, did. After publishing one of the books in her AMNAR series, she received an extensive commentary and critique from a reader. Most writers would be somewhere between put off or downright offended. Not Black—she was grateful. Her readers, she believes, are hardcore epic fantasy readers, spending huge amounts of time devouring nearly everything written in the genre, far more than she could possibly read. Over a period of years, some of these fans had become so well versed in what makes epic fantasy read extraordinarily well that their insights become as valuable as those of the best editors. When such readers take the time to share detailed feedback and recommendations on better ways to structure a plot or create a character, Black believes that as an author, you'd be silly not to at least listen. She quickly realized how much better the "offending" book would read if she acted upon the advice of this one reader. She went back and rewrote the already published book and rereleased it to a much friendlier reception.

Filmmakers Tim Burton and Ridley Scott recently brought their audiences onboard at the very beginning of their creation process, turning to their tribes, viewers, and readers to help them co-create works.

In July 2010, Ridley Scott and director Kevin Macdonald teamed with YouTube.com to create *Life in a Day*, the first user-generated feature-length documentary. The idea was to feature a single day, July 24, 2010, in the lives of people from all over the world, as filmed through the lenses of their own cameras. Entrants were asked to shoot footage that explored three questions: what do you fear, what do you love, and what makes you laugh? By the July 31, 2010, deadline, more than 80,000 people had uploaded more than 4,500 hours of footage. Scott and Macdonald then molded these submissions into a documentary film that premiered at the Sundance Film Festival in January 2011. Individual clips and the documentary can be viewed on the Life in a Day channel at youtube.com/lifeinaday.

Shortly after, Tim Burton brought together the public reach of Twitter and the story-creation method, originated by the French Surrealists, called Cadavre Exquis ("exquisite corpse"), in which a group of people write a story, one taking up where the last left off. Between November 22 and December 6, 2010, Burton asked his Twitter followers to co-create a new story about his character Stainboy. Followers posted potential "next sentences" that picked up from the prior day's sentence along with a hashtag to identify story submissions. At the end of each day, Burton selected the best submission and added it to the story. In the end, he chose submissions from eighty-eight people and gave credit to each for their contributions to the final work (which you can read at burtonstory.com/connect.php).

Driving all of these examples are two giant changes. One is the ability to tap technology to make the process markedly easier than it would have been even a few years ago, when many of these community-involved creations simply could not have happened. The second is a massive shift in the psychology of creation on two levels: the willingness to elevate the consumer to the role of co-creator, and the willingness to share creative credit in exchange for a better, faster outcome and a process that engages fans right from the start.

YOU STILL NEED TO LEAD

As we saw earlier, whether you're tapping a full-blown lean creation process—with rapid prototyping, iteration, and co-creation—or focusing more on just the co-creation aspect, it's important to preserve your role as the leader and primary visionary in the process. As Henry Ford famously said, "If I had asked people what they wanted, they would have said faster horses." You still need to bring the original big idea to the table, set the tone and expectations, and control the pace and level of influence your end users have. That means keeping your finger on the pulse of the project's creative evolution and finding the sweet spot where you have enough contributions to improve what you're creating and to humanize the process, but not so much that the vision becomes diluted and the process devolves into chaos.

You can't surrender the process entirely to the community. While science and process are valuable adjuncts, intuition and experience still count. Your community, while capable of helping you refine what you're creating, may not be able to uncover an entirely different idea that may be an order of magnitude better. If as a creative leader you feel the process isn't giving you the result you need, you may have to revisit the "big idea" side of the equation yet again.

To do all of this, you need to have a strong sense of what you're trying to build, whom you're serving, and why. Otherwise you risk diluting your quest and creative output. Input and insight are great, but they're not a replacement for strong leadership and vision. Co-creation is a tool that's best tapped to inform your creation, not run it.

BEWARE THE CO-CREATION CRUTCH

You must also be alert to the lure of leaning on the crowd as a crutch to protect yourself emotionally from the pain of being the sole owner of a creative failure. Ask whether you're leveraging the creative power of others as a tool or as a buffer. If you find yourself relying on the crowd not only to inform but to guide your direction, that's a major sign that you're yielding autonomy and vision to others.

That bad move is most often an attempt to shield yourself from the potential pain of fully owning a failed attempt. You're using co-creation as a crutch to avoid risking fear and uncertainty in the name of creating genius. Creating extraordinary output requires you to give everything you have. Bringing other people in does not lessen that burden, nor does it allow you the leeway to blame them for a failed effort. It simply provides a greater set of data points, constructive judgment, and a higher level of incremental certainty.

Co-creation raises a few big questions.

WHO GETS THE CREDIT?

There is a tremendous amount of ego driving the world of creation. Many of us are motivated not just by the need to create something brilliant, but by the desire to be recognized for our genius. The impulse to want approval may be the dark underbelly of the creative process, but the truth is we're all driven to create by some blend of wanting to make an impact and provide a useful service, the need for personal expression, and our own irrepressible ego.

Like it or not, a part of our drive to create will always be ego. In some fields creators have a huge amount of status and even income tied up in who gets credit when things go right. If you work for a creative agency, you want your name to be on the big wins, because credit begets power, money, and choice.

What happens when you bring the idea of end-user co-creation into this process? What if you are a creative director who brings to market a hugely successful interactive project or campaign that was built by you, your immediate team . . . and the 10,000 people who shared ideas and insights as you iterated the project? You get more certainty and interaction along the way, leading to a higher likelihood of success, but you've also given up a certain amount of the claim to being the sole genius behind the effort.

That idea terrifies some traditional creators who've built careers as chosen ones. A new breed of creators who add the power of co-creation—who learn the new skill of leading, filtering, curating, and synthesizing—are already sharing the stage with the traditional solo creative visionaries. The impact of this new way of working will continue to grow as co-creators prove themselves able to offer consistently better creations and outcomes in a fraction of the time and with less waste.

WHAT ABOUT CREATIVE DILUTION?

One criticism of co-creation, which comes up most often in the realm of the more traditional creative art forms, is that the co-creation process is merely creating art by committee. With rare exceptions, this calamitous practice yields mediocre dreck—an undistinguished collision of noise, ideas, compromise, sacrifice, and a lack of vision and leadership. It happens, a lot, but it's not inevitable.

One of the most prolific dance choreographers who's ever lived, Twyla Tharp, wrote an entire book about the value of collaborative creation—*The Collaborative Habit* (2009)—in which she talks about the importance of working with others as essential in all but the smallest of endeavors. Some of the greatest comedy comes from the spontaneous improvisation between solo geniuses riffing along with each other "within an agreed upon framework" that gives the work momentum and keeps it building, rather than tearing itself down. Many great painters and writers bring others in to comment on and share criticisms and insights about their work while it's still in progress.

This type of co-creation doesn't seem all that threatening to the traditional artist because the co-creators are perceived to be "at their level." What does seem offensive is the notion of elevating the contributions of "mere consumers" to the level of worthy co-creators.

If you're creating solely because you must create, without the desire to exchange value for your creations, by all means let your muse be your guide. Do it because your creation is an expression of your soul, because it simply must be done. But the moment you create with the expectation and the desire to be paid for your work, other people matter. Not just other artists. Other people who would enjoy, experience, and buy your work. You may not want to bring them into the creative process, but the moment you ask them to help pay your rent, they're in, whether you say they are or not. You determine whether you're being true to your muse. But they determine whether that truth gets expressed full-time or on weekends and evenings, after your day job ends.

In early 2010 Steven Pressfield, author of *The War of Art, The Legend of Bagger Vance*, and numerous other books that have been hugely successful in both a critical and commercial sense, penned a blog post about how he chooses his projects. At first, back when he was a younger screenwriter, it was largely about commercial success, and it emptied him out. Then he pursued the sweet spot between what he wanted to create in his heart and what he thought could make money. That didn't work either. So he decided to, in his words, "get stupid and jump off a cliff" and write only what he felt he had to write, without regard for whether his readers would want to read it. That was the moment when he broke through and his career took off.

Steve remains committed to this approach, although he confessed to me that if he truly believed a project had zero commercial appeal, he'd have to weigh it pretty seriously, especially because in his mind, each new book is a two- to three-year commitment.

I asked Seth Godin, a good friend of Pressfield's, for his take on Steve's commercial-prospects-be-damned approach. He argued that creating something commercial that appeals to the desires of your tribe isn't necessarily a compromise. As he told me:

> If you view this as an opportunity and not an obligation, then you're going to want to seek out creative opportunities that will give you the chance to have more creative opportunities. And thus, picking something that's going to work in the marketplace is not a compromise because working in the marketplace is the best chance that you have to be able to do it again.
>
> Many times we trick ourselves. Sometimes we trick ourselves by saying, "I'm doing this super commercial thing 'cause that's what I'm supposed to do." And then we create a work that's banal and of course it fails. I think we do that on purpose because it's safer to do something that's going to fail. The alternative, also a mistake, is we pick something that's super not commercial, that we know is going to fail. Because, again, it's safer than picking something that might resonate with an audience. . . .
>
> Steve has created work that's outside the realm of what would be expected. But he certainly has created work that has resonated with the market. And I think he has been able to do that because he has confronted his fear of shipping something that people might notice.

Creating work that brings in others and appeals to them is not the functional equivalent of censoring your work. It doesn't mean you become an artistic dog on a collector's leash. It means you choose work that you believe you can be true to, but that the market will also value and allow you to do more of.

DOES CO-CREATION PROHIBIT TASTEMAKING?

Maybe bringing your users into the creative process or weighing their preferences won't bastardize the process by default, but doesn't it kill your ability to take your audience to a place they've not yet gone? To not just serve their current tastes and preferences but to lead them to entirely new ones?

The short answer is maybe, but not because of the co-creation.

One of the key roles of creators in society has been to push people beyond their comfort zones. They create new experiences that expose their audiences not just to the creator's take on the current zeitgeist, but to the possibility of an entirely new worldview and experience.

As part of the creative process, relying too much on the input of potential consumers brings with it the very real risk that you will lose your ability to lead people to a new place. A huge part of your challenge as a creator is to live outside the comfort zone of the known and familiar. This entire book is about harnessing the discomfort that is part of that journey. It's hard for *you* to do it, of course, but you can be sure the followers and consumers of your creations will resist your attempt to dismantle their cozy little "life as I know it" boxes with zest.

Whether you do it in collaborative bits or through bold finished works, it takes a massive amount of will, fortification, and leadership to knock people off their stools and open them up to a different take on the world. Either way, you still need to own that challenge.

The argument against bringing users into the process of creation isn't really about how it may stop you from being a tastemaker or paradigm-shifter. What it's really about is whether you have the will to lead people to that new place, regardless of the point in the process when you grant them access.

As Mahatma Gandhi said, "First they ignore you, then they laugh at you, then they fight you, then you win." In bits or in bursts, you will need the will to endure, to educate, and to lead.

SHOULD CO-CREATORS GET VALUE FOR THEIR INPUT?

This question has sparked a raging debate in the world of co-creation. Should those who contribute feedback, insight, ideas, and value to your project be entitled to some value for their input?

Of course they should. How to define and allocate value, however, is something unique to each creator, tribe, and dynamic. If you're asking for value, you should offer something of value in exchange. That doesn't automatically mean money; it could be access, engagement, information, or anything deemed a worthy compensation for the effort of your co-creators. But there should be something.

This issue came up in the context of titling this book. As I've mentioned, while working on the manuscript, I created a private creation tribe. About a month later, I e-mailed the tribe to ask if they'd share their thoughts on a bunch of title and subtitle options. I added a space for anyone who wanted to share additional insights or any titles that came to them. The response was substantial, the reception was fantastic, and many had a lot of fun with the process; in short, my creation tribe readily shared insights and ideas. Then a single anonymous comment came in: "Isn't that the kind of thing people get paid to do? It's crazymaking that personal dev bloggers keep trying to use their platform for unpaid help."

I was aghast at the accusation that I was getting more than I was giving. I know the arguments about spec work, creatives, and contests this person was referring to. But that's not what my creation tribe was about, nor is it what happens in a genuine user co-creation environment.

When people raised their hands to join my creation tribe, they were also agreeing to a bargain. I promised to grant them increased access to me, to my process, ideas, insights, and thoughts on both the book and the publishing process in general. I committed to go even further, conducting educational live Q&A calls with them (ones that I'd get paid serious money to lead publicly), during which I shared all sorts of information about writing, publishing, marketing, and living the writer's life. In exchange for that, I told them I would occasionally ask for their insights and opinions on my creation. That was the bargain. It was important to me that everyone who joined was offered and felt they were getting value in exchange for their involvement in the creative journey.

This is similar to the bargain made with alpha and beta testing communities for technology and games. Users get early access to the coolest new experiences in exchange for their help in identifying and resolving bugs and sharing how they think the experiences could be improved. It's like the basic idea of the online encyclopedia Wikipedia: millions of users contribute time, insight, information, and energy in exchange for knowing they helped bring something amazing to life. That same bargain unfolds, albeit at a far more rapid pace, in the world of lean creation. Access—and, at times, credit—are offered in exchange for participation and insight.

In most endeavors that are in part fueled by co-creation, users are given value in a currency that works for them. That's not to say it always happens this way. But it was important for me to base my process on what I believed to be a bargain that gave not just equal but more value to those who agreed to share the journey with me.

DOES A LEAN OR CO-CREATION
APPROACH WORK FOR EVERYONE?

Yes. And no.

Around the time I was finishing the manuscript for this book, I began to realize how much of my life I was spending in front of a screen. It really bothered me. For a good part of my earlier life, I'd been a painter, musician, builder, and entrepreneur. I love to get my hands dirty. I love to create things I can touch, feel, play with, hear, see, and point to (sadly, I'm still woefully attached to my ego). I also play guitar and have always loved the physical form of guitars—electric, acoustic, and classical. So I committed to reallocating some of my energy in the coming year to getting my hands back into a tangible craft. I wanted to learn the art of lutherie, or guitar building. As I explored the process, I began to wonder whether building something as personal and individually crafted as a guitar (it takes two to six months for a single guitar to reach its final form) could benefit from this process. I extended the question out from there. Could a solo painter or sculptor, whose works might take months or years to envision and manifest in final form, benefit from the change in certainty and fear that a lean/co-creation process might bring? Or were some things just too individualized and sacred? The answer to both questions is yes.

The truth is, anyone who creates anything and then seeks value in exchange for that creation ends up integrating the feedback of buyers, whether he or she realizes it or not. The process just gets extended out over time. It happens over the course of a body of work or career rather than within the creation of a single work. Iterations take months or years instead of minutes or days. The information we get in response to our creations serves to both guide each new iteration or individual work of creation and helps us answer the second giant question I introduced earlier in the book: Am *I* good enough?

We are always seeking certainty and trying to alleviate the judgment we anticipate and the accompanying risk of loss by asking for input. The challenge, as we've seen, is that as a solo creator seeking input, you don't have the benefit of a team that can more quickly tell you whether you're using the desire for input and approval as an excuse for inaction or a source of evolutionary creation. This is where creating strong feedback mechanisms, rituals, and judgment-leveling creation hives becomes immensely important to the endeavor.

WHAT ABOUT APPLE?

If this is the future of creation, then why does one of the most consistently innovative, paradigm-crushing companies on the planet operate in seemingly utter secrecy, without releasing even so much as a screenshot of a product until launch day? Good question, glad you asked.

A caveat: Because of that veil of secrecy, those who haven't been on the inside don't actually know how the company operates. But there are several interesting things about Apple.

First, it's led by a team of some of the most innovative and creative leaders on the planet, people who have made careers doing what nobody else has done. Second, it's big. As of September 2010, Apple reported approximately 46,600 employees. Third, a huge percentage of its employees are very likely hard-core organic users of the company's consumer-oriented products. These three facts allow Apple to create its own entirely internal lean creative ecosystem—prototyping, releasing, soliciting feedback, and iterating rapidly without needing to rely on an external community of users. Also, like many other tech companies, once products are released and feedback is given, many features are eventually incoporated in future public versions.

PUTTING IT TOGETHER

While there is no way to remove uncertainty from the process of creation, technology is now opening doors that allow us to reallocate how and when we experience that uncertainty. It lets us bring legitimate feedback from those for whom we create into the process earlier and more often. But as we've seen, with this potential evolution in creative process comes a new set of responsibilities and questions. Here are a few critical places to keep your focus as you explore this new dynamic:

Shift Your Focus to Learning

One of the big leaps Eric Ries suggested entrepreneurs take is to focus less on traffic, sales, or profits and more on learning as much as possible as quickly as possible.

Explore Your MVP

Ask yourself whether you can create a minimum viable product that is finished enough to be able to release so you can gather feedback that you can incorporate in the next iteration.

Be Open to Collaboration with Colleagues and End Users

If you are creating simply because that is why you are here, without reference to whether your output will ever earn enough to let you live well in the world, it's easier to create in a vacuum. However, the moment you seek money in exchange for your creation, the opinions of your eventual buyers matter. Own that and bring them into the process on whatever level you feel comfortable.

Bring Out Your Leader

Bringing others into the process requires a set of skills that many creators either don't normally exercise or haven't fully developed, the most important involving leadership. You'll need to be ready to step up and guide those who are kind enough to join in the endeavor with you and, at times, even go against them when your gut tells you there's a much bigger, better idea or solution that you're all missing.

Explore Your Value Exchange

If you are asking something from others, explore what type of value you can offer in exchange.

Until now, we've focused largely on changes to the creation environment and work-flow process as a way to make it easier to embrace the risk, exposure, and uncertainty that accompanies any endeavor and often leads to intolerable levels of anxiety and fear. Now it's time to shift the focus a bit and explore a series of personal practices that, intelligently leveraged, can transform the way we experience the creative process.

7

TRAIN YOUR BRAIN

FEAR INTO FUEL

REMEMBER RANDY KOMISAR, the lawyer turned CEO turned Virtual CEO, author, professor, and now venture capitalist? Many would call his extraordinary ability to continually shift shapes, then dominate a God-given gift. They might say he's a born fear alchemist. Not so. While acknowledging that he believed he was likely "wired" to handle fear and uncertainty better than most, Komisar credits not so much his genetics, but his spiritual practice as a source of both creative solace and deep psychological power. "When you step into ambiguity and uncertainty, when you surround yourself essentially with uncertainty without a life jacket," Komisar told me, "you still have to have a foundation, a core, a center. You can't be completely relative in that environment. . . . Even though you may not actually have a clear objective and you certainly don't have a path to get there, you have to have a keel that keeps you centered. Spiritual practice allowed me to find that keel."

Komisar tried meditating during law school, but it didn't take, though he'd always been interested in Eastern philosophy. "Equanimity," he said, "is a powerful muscle if you're going to step into the ambiguous void." That interest eventually led him to study Zen Buddhism. Over the years, his practice evolved from a sense of trying to understand to a sense of trying to realize and largely moved from reading and lectures and retreats to the purity of meditation. He's meditated every day since he met his teacher in 1995.

Listening to Komisar's exaltation of his meditation, mindfulness, and spiritual practice, you'd think you were listening not to one of the most acclaimed entrepreneurs and venture capitalists in the Valley, but rather to a painter, poet, or writer. Indeed in my many conversations with more traditional creators, similar practices were not unusual. During our conversation, Komisar added:

> It's a process of stripping myself bare of all of the pressures, all of the barnacles that accumulate around you every day as you interact in the world—the pressures, the expectations, the ego, the things that ultimately make your vision unclear. And every day, my meditation is about moving those, getting absolutely clearer in that moment and open, allowing myself to open back up, to walk out into the world and have it happen all over again.

What's fascinating about his practice is how he identifies it as his keel, the point at which he feels always tethered to the ground; his practice provides him with an anchor that allows the rest of him to take action in the face of fear and uncertainty. Komisar's spiritual practice is a highly specialized example of the certainty anchors we explored earlier. But the power of this particular type of certainty anchor extends far beyond the grounding effect of routine.

Meditation, mindfulness, and many forms of contemplation-driven spiritual practice are examples of something called attentional training (AT), practices that either innately or by will require intense,

focused awareness. Through daily repetition, they create both physiological and psychological changes that can profoundly alter the way
we experience and handle nearly any challenge or endeavor. AT is not
only a way, as Randy put it, to "touch stone"; it also opens up channels
to insight and innovation.

Denver-based Sonia Simone knows this all too well. When she
worked for small, often tech-driven companies, she revealed to
me, "there was always somebody else taking the risks and shaping the
vision for the company, and I was always the helper and that was sort
of how I thought about myself. And over time, companies get bought
and they get investors and all the awesome things that brought you to
the company start to get really screwed up and ugly and stupid and
wrongheaded. And so after this happened to me for the third time, I
just got fed up with it."

Wanting more control over her career, Simone took the advice of
her friend Josh Kaufman, author of *The Personal MBA* (2010), and
started reading her way into the knowledge she needed. Simone
devoured business book after book and blog after blog. Then, instead of finding a higher-level position at a bigger company, she chose
a different path. She blended what she was learning with twenty
years of in-house marketing experience and launched her own marketing blog and consulting and writing business, *Remarkable-
Communication.com*.

Remarkable Communication grew on the side for the next year
and a half and put her onto the radar of uber-blogger Brian Clark,
who founded *Copyblogger.com*. Simone began to post weekly on
Copyblogger. She's now a partner in Copyblogger Media, an expanded,
multi-tentacled, highly successful interactive endeavor that runs a
variety of content assets, training programs, and products. And she
did all of this with a baby at home and a husband who was a stay-at-
home dad, positioning her as the sole breadwinner in the family. As
she told me:

There is definitely part of my emotional makeup that would love it if I could just relax and let some kind of benevolent, all-powerful parent take care of me. I would love that. But I don't have that. . . . There's no such thing as some all-powerful person or organization or institution, unless you are in prison, that's going to take care of you. It doesn't exist. So Santa Claus is not real and you grieve that for a bit, but you kind of knew it anyway. . . . You're shaking off all of the constriction that you've been living in and all this bubble wrap and you walk out and it's painful, but it's more interesting than painful.

Simone's ability to view her headlong dive into creating a new company, life, and living as painful, but "more interesting than painful" was not something that came easily or naturally. It was acquired through effort. Meditation had formed the centerpiece of her creative life for decades. She considers it the most essential thing she does in her business, but for a different reason than Komisar. "When you sit," shared Simone, "you learn to drop. You still have states, and they still come up, and they're still very powerful . . . but it gives you the ability to feel it, and then say, 'Could I drop that? Maybe not the state but the story line.'"

Practicing and mastering that one skill—touching, then dropping your current thought pattern—is hugely important for any creator. Things always happen that knock you off the rails, and if you become unhinged every time, your endeavor will be short-lived. "You still have emotions," added Simone, "and you still laugh and you still have a great sense of humor, and you still get pissed off and you still just hate people sometimes." But you learn to let go of them and refocus rather than fester in them.

Palo Alto Software founder Tim Berry shared a similar awakening with me about his mindfulness-based AT practice, "I always needed to pull out of the stream," he said. "I have helicopter mind . . . but [through my practice] . . . immediately I recognize helicopter mind versus quiet mind and I've always needed to find that quiet place where I can unconsciously sort things through and let my different thoughts settle."

Addressing an audience of film students at Boston's Majestic Theater, filmmaker David Lynch pointed to yet another form of AT—Transcendental Meditation—as the source of deep calm and tremendous leaps in creativity. "Anger and depression and sorrow, they're beautiful things in a story," he said with the audience, "but they're like a poison to the filmmaker, they're a poison to the painter, they're a poison to creativity." Through his practice, he added, "the enjoyment of life grows. Huge ideas flow more. Everybody has more fun on the set. Creativity flows."

WHAT EXACTLY IS ATTENTIONAL TRAINING?

Attentional training (AT) is a catch-all phrase for a wide variety of techniques that create certain psychological and physiological changes in your body and brain. Many of them are derived from centuries-old ideologies and philosophies; some have religious overlays, while others have always been more secular. Major approaches include:

- Active AT
- Guided Meditation
- Transcendental Meditation
- Insight meditation
- Mindfulness
- Zen meditation and zazen
- Buddhist meditation
- Mantra meditation
- Chanting and prayer across many traditions

- Biofeedback
- Hypnosis and self-hypnosis

Each approach is built around a set of relatively simple daily practices. The common element is the experience of focused awareness for a committed period of time, which can be as little as a few minutes a day or as long as days or even weeks. Sometimes the focus is internal—for example, on the sensations of the breath or the repetition of sounds. At other times, it's external, with a more diffused focus on your environment. And there are approaches that integrate both. Sometimes a great deal of deliberate effort is required to focus the mind, at least in the beginning, while certain other approaches, in which intense focus is an automatic part of the process, draw the mind into a place of deep attention with far less effort. We'll focus on three widely practiced approaches that do a great job of spanning the gaps between these approaches and between Western science and modern-day spiritual practice.

1. Active AT

This is how the vast majority of people get their AT in. Many of us invoke the major elements of AT, without even realizing it, as we engage in specific types of sports and pursue serious hobbies like painting, composing or playing music, knitting, or outdoor activities. The two expressions of this approach tend to be found in activities that are either:

- driven by novelty, speed, and an extended, intense state of concentration that is "imposed without effort" by the requirements of the activity, or
- repetitive, deliberate, and done in an environment that provokes

comfort, lowers your guard, and does not require vigilant attention to rapidly changing circumstances, allowing you to melt into that elusive "zone" state.

An example of the first is trail running, which requires intense observation, concentration, and adjustment to a rapidly changing, high-alert environment; track or quiet road running is an example of the second. The point is, the right kind of physical activity can induce the AT state. And over time that psycho-physiological training filters past your physical health to your mind-set and creativity. But all active AT is not created equal.

I've always been someone who finds that special place through intense, solitary, rapidly changing movement. Activities like mountain biking quickly on a narrow, winding, wooded track or trail running drop me into a place of hyperfocus. The world around me or beyond the trail ahead ceases to exist. I don't have to work to make that happen; it just does: the constant rapid changes in environment demand my absolute attention.

However, I've also found that, as enjoyable as they are, activities that by their very nature demand hyperfocus don't cultivate the same sense of stillness, clarity, insight, and space that "stiller," more repetitive types of moving or sitting AT allow.

Mountain biking gets me one level deep, but a sixty-mile road ride on a barely trafficked country loop or a long hike on a well-graded, nontechnical mountain trail provides the opportunity to go to a very different place. Without worrying about lots of traffic, trees, roots, rocks, and critters flying into me, I can drop into the rhythm of my feet and my breath much more deeply. My mind has to work a lot less. That's the place where the chatter isn't overpowered by rapid-fire change and intense attention; instead it's diminished by the rhythm of the movement. That one difference creates a profound change in experience, because instead of filling my head space, it clears it. That's the place where the pain of creation begins to ease and in which insights and ideas arrive like manna from creation heaven.

After years of resistance, I've also found that a sitting AT practice delivers benefits that extend beyond those experienced through a purely moving practice. Many of those benefits are described in the next two sections.

2. Mindfulness and "Ambient" AT

Originally derived from Buddhism, the term "mindfulness" has become largely diluted. These days it serves as a bit of a catchall phrase for an approach to AT from the Tibetan lineage to Zen to Insight, Vipassana, and the more Western-minded, ideology-free Mindfulness-Based Stress Reduction developed by Jon Kabat-Zinn. There are, however, very real differences in practice, and the ideologies that wrap around the core practices can vary quite dramatically, based on both the teachings and the individual teachers' interpretations. For our purposes, we'll keep the focus nondogmatic, streamlined, and practical.

Mindfulness is, most broadly, an approach to how you exist in the world. Sitting and walking meditation are common daily practices, but mindfulness is also about how you wash your dishes, do your work, talk to people, and engage with the world. It's not about seeking to create change; it's about being with what you have and where you are, in the moment, every moment. Rather than focusing and excluding, it's about resting a smallish bit of attention on your breath, then progressively opening to anything and everything that's happening around you.

The real challenge in the practice lies in letting go of new sensations and thoughts as they come and bringing yourself back to the breath and the moment. It's a practice steeped in new beginnings. This is the "dropping" practice Sonia Simone spoke of. You become more aware of the moments when your mind wanders off, note the departure, let go of the thought or sensation your mind was playing with, then begin again. This may happen hundreds of times in a single session. The immediate inclination (at least mine) is to get annoyed at the utter lack of control you have over your attention. But you quickly learn that such wanderings are okay, even expected. You start to view them not as a good thing or a bad thing, but just a thing. They're simply an expected part of how our minds work. Rather than fight it, you open to it, acknowledge it, and come back.

Mindfulness meditation is the basis of Jon Kabat-Zinn's Mindfulness-Based Stress Reduction (MBSR) protocol, as well as the follow-on protocol known as Mindfulness-Based Cognitive Therapy. Because they are relatively standardized, nondogmatic, and clinically grounded, MBSR and its variations are well-documented and well-researched approaches that are being heavily studied today. Beyond fostering an enhanced ability to return to work and begin again after lapses in attention or battles with resistance, as many studies demonstrate, MBSR has also been shown to create measurable positive changes in both momentary and sustained brain states, in our moods and health, in our cognitive and physiological states, and even in neuron density.

3. Transcendental Meditation and Mantra-based Meditation

Transcendental Meditation was introduced to the world by Maharishi Mahesh Yogi some fifty years ago. According to TM.org, "During the past 50 years, more than five million people have learned the Transcendental Meditation technique and . . . Maharishi has trained over 40,000 teachers, opened thousands of teaching centers, and founded hundreds of schools, colleges and universities." It is the most widely practiced and probably the most standardized teaching and practice protocol around today.

Derived from Vedic traditions and teachings, TM is an adaptation of mantra meditation, which focuses on the repetition of a sound that is "given" to you by a teacher to create a state of inward focus and calm. Though rooted in a decidedly spiritual beginning, over the decades TM has taken on a more Western, science-driven tone, though it's ideological roots still form the basis of the practice and the broader movement. It is a heavily researched approach; hundreds of studies on it have been published. Over the past few years, though, mindfulness seems to be the focus of much of the academic research.

TM instruction is highly standardized into a seven-session training sequence. Everyone learns the same thing, and training is readily available in many places. Once you learn it, you practice twice a day for twenty minutes at a time. David Lynch has become a huge proponent of TM practice as a tool for creators, because it cultivates a shift in brain coherence, mood, and the ability to lean into fear and uncertainty, and allows you to tap what the TM community calls the Unified Field, a form of shared consciousness that can become a rich source of creative insight.

That last part may sound a bit out there, but there's actually some science behind it. In a study reported in the *Journal of Creative Behavior* in 1979 that used the Torrance Test of Creative Thinking to measure figural and verbal creativity, TM practitioners scored significantly higher than a control group on critical measures of creativity.

Beyond creativity, the mind-set benefits of TM and other mantra-based approaches to AT are real and well documented—real enough for top C-suite executives and corporate leaders, from former Medtronics CEO Bill George to Def Jam co-founder Russell Simmons, to point to it as a source of tremendous calm in their very stressful lives. As Lynch noted, it's not unusual to experience a fairly immediate effect (often within days) that then deepens over time.

You may also want to explore the variety of similar mantra-based approaches to AT, available through a wide range of centers, teachers, yoga studios, and even online programs. As with any approach, explore with an open mind and ask a lot of questions.

Not Just for the Experimental Crowd

If this book were being written forty years ago, you'd have to take on faith the claims of those quirky people who swear by AT as a source of humanity, sanity, and creativity. For hundreds and, for some approaches, thousands of years, these practices have endured based on blind faith and some fairly mystical claims, bundled with generations of anecdotal evidence. But touched off by the investigations of Harvard Medical School professor Herbert Benson in the 1970s, there is now an admirable body of science substantiating many of the claims (levitation and enlightenment aside).

In 1979 one of Benson's protégés, Jon Kabat-Zinn, began offering at the University of Massachusetts Medical School an eight-week protocol called Mindfulness-Based Stress Reduction, based on the core nonideological mindfulness practices from Buddhism. To date, tens of thousands of people have completed his program, and the "mindset" results have been nothing short of stunning, especially when it comes to mood, anxiety, stress, and sleep.

Research conducted in 1991 jointly by the Dalai Lama and Richard Davidson, Director of the University of Wisconsin's Waisman Laboratory for Brain Imaging and Behavior, confirmed and expanded Zinn's research, studying the effect on fairly new or "lay" meditators as well as on Tibetan Buddhist monks who had been practicing many hours a day for years or decades.

Researcher Sara Lazar, PhD, of the Psychiatric Neuroimaging Research Program at Massachusetts General Hospital, then picked up the mindfulness meditation science ball and ran even further in 2005. Her research, funded by the National Institutes of Health and the Centers for Disease Control, revealed measurable physical changes in the brains of people who meditated that reached beyond the actual bout of meditation to create "a serious impact on your brain long beyond the time when you're actually sitting and meditating."

In a study whose results were published in the January 30, 2011, issue of *Psychiatry Research: Neuroimaging*, Lazar led a team that followed participants in Kabat-Zinn's eight-week MBSR program; the researchers used magnetic resonance imaging to measure significant changes in the brain, specifically in the amygdala, a brain region that is integrally involved in fear and anxiety. This was the first study to correlate this form of AT with not only behavioral and psychological but also structural changes in the brain that help explain various outward effects.

Similarly, numerous published studies on TM point to its exceptional effectiveness in countering anxiety; in recent years, an increasing number of studies have also focused on the effects of TM on cognitive function and creativity.

Science, it appears, is revealing a neurological basis for the experiences shared by Komisar, Simone, Lynch, and millions of others. AT drops you into a place that, as your practice deepens, increasingly inoculates you against much of the pain and suffering that accompanies scenarios that would normally bring on fear, uncertainty, and anxiety. It doesn't change the scenario. It doesn't alter your circumstance. It doesn't make things more certain or less fearful or pull you out of the state you need to be in in order to create. It just changes the way you live in this place. It allows you the equanimity to lean into uncertainty, risk, and judgment with greater ease. The deeper down the AT rabbit hole you go, the stronger AT's effect and the more it pervades not just the period during and immediately surrounding the actual practice, but every moment of every day.

This alone is transformative for the artist, entrepreneur, or organization-level innovator, but that's still not the full picture. For me, as well as every other creator I've met who engages in some form of AT practice, it does one other mission-critical thing: Attentional training provides fertile ground for the incubation of big ideas. Many of the greatest insights come when you step away and completely unplug. At the moment you find enough stillness for the chatter that fills your head all day long to drop away, revelation begins to sneak in. Insights and big world-changing ideas effervesce into existence. AT is potentially the single greatest tool for insight and ideation ever created. For anyone on a quest to create something brilliant from nothing, its importance could not be greater.

Can Anyone Learn AT?

As someone who has explored a variety of approaches to AT over the years and has spent seven years teaching yoga and a variety of approaches to AT to thousands of people, including other teachers, I've seen the process of raised eyebrows, skeptical trial, increased commitment, and "Wow, it works" too many times to recount.

Even after being presented with a mountain of anecdotal evidence and a growing body of hard science, two objections never seem to fade.

- It takes too long to work.
- I've tried and tried and I just can't meditate.

Let's talk about these, one at a time.

It Takes Too Long to Work

I always think it's funny when someone who's willing to wait years to see a dime from a start-up, months to finish a painting, years to complete a book, and decades to create a body of work fabricates the belief that something as potentially life and work altering as AT takes too long to work for them to commit to it.

Let's do a bit of myth busting here. Yes, the benefits of AT will deepen over time. They'll continue to deepen years or decades later. For most people, ten minutes a day, every day will lead to noticeable effects faster than five minutes every other day. This is a practice that you build gradually over the course of your entire life.

That said, there's some pretty fascinating new research that has blown the lid off the assumption that it takes a least a few months of daily practice before you will experience measurable change. In 2007, a joint project, conducted by Professor Yi-Yuan Tang of Dalian University of Technology and Professor Michael Posner of the University of Oregon, reported that just five days of a meditation-based form of AT called Integrative Body Mind Technique (IBMT) led to "low levels of the stress hormone cortisol among Chinese students." The experimental group also showed lower levels of anxiety, depression, anger, and fatigue than students in a group practicing a nonmeditative form of relaxation. Building on this work, in 2010 Yi-Yuan Tang and Posner published a follow-up study in the *Proceedings of the National Academy of Sciences* reporting on research that involved forty-five University of Oregon students. Twenty-two subjects received training in IBMT, while twenty-three participants were in a control group that received the same amount of nonmeditative relaxation training. Brain-imaging equipment revealed structural changes only in the IBMT subjects' brains, and in as little as six hours.

Moreover, a study by Professor Fadel Zeidan and his team at the Department of Neurobiology and Anatomy, Wake Forest University School of Medicine, reported in *Consciousness and Cognition*, revealed that four days of mindfulness training "reduced fatigue, anxiety, and increased mindfulness. Moreover, brief mindfulness training significantly improved visuo-spatial processing, working memory, and executive functioning." What we're seeing in this most recent wave of research is serious compression in the amount of time and practice required for measurable benefit. That compression is being reported anecdotally and measured and reported in clinical, published, peer-reviewed studies. While the benefits probably deepen over a period of months and years, the research clearly shows very real, very measurable effect in a matter of days.

A major word of caution: AT, as taught in nearly every tradition, eschews a focus on goals and expectations. Here's where it gets really delicate. In our world, nobody sits in AT just for the purpose of sitting in AT. Time is our most precious asset. If we give it up, even a few minutes of it, we want something out of it. Guaranteed. That's why we do it.

But the result of attentional training is correctly pursued "without attachment"—which means you practice with the intention of practicing, knowing that it will lead you closer to a state you aspire to attain, but without the express goal of producing forward movement toward that place every time you sit in AT. The only commitment or expectation you bring to your practice on any given day is to practice. To be present. Because the moment you start setting goals for additional benefits that are attached to each practice, you start to bring expectations and judgment to your practice that take you out of the state you're working so hard to explore.

Difficult though it may be, while there's no doubt we're all doing this for a reason, when you come to the mat, the chair, or wherever else you practice, you need to leave any expectation about results at the door. If you bring them in, you essentially guarantee not only frustration along the way, but a far higher likelihood you'll quit shortly after you begin. You'll lose all the potential benefits before you even start.

I Just Can't Meditate

Oy, do I feel your pain! Approaches to AT in which the nature of the practice intrinsically requires focus tend to be far easier to master. When I mountain bike on winding trails through trees, I need to stay intensely focused. Repetition of a sound, word, prayer, or chant also requires a certain amount of automatic focus. If your mind wanders off, the repetition and the rhythm stop. Other approaches, such as mindfulness, require more effort. Regardless of the approach, anyone can learn and develop a daily AT practice. It took me years to realize the following:

- There is no single right or wrong way to do AT. If you commit to sit for ten minutes and every second your mind swings violently between thinking about a million different things and chastising yourself for thinking about a million different things when you're supposed to be focusing, you're still doing it right. That's just part of the process. Think of your brain as a puppy. You'd never expect to be able to train a puppy in one sitting. It takes time. It's the same with your brain.
- That magical, brightly lit, out-of-body experience you've seen in the movies very likely isn't going to happen (though it may on occasion). No matter what does happen, there's a pretty good chance you're still doing it right and getting something out of it.
- Even ADD-addled, creative types on hyperdrive, like me, can build a serious practice. In fact, the more easily distracted you are, the more beneficial an AT practice will be.
- It's not about time served. While some approaches, like TM, ask you to commit to a fairly rigid twenty minutes twice a day, many other approaches allow for a gentler easing into the process. A few minutes a day is a good beginning for many. Start with three to five, then add two minutes a week. One of the techniques

that's worked best in helping me extend my time sitting is to simply commit to five to ten minutes. Inevitably, I find myself settling in and wanting more, but had I committed to a thirty-minute practice from the beginning, I never would have sat to start with.

You may already have the beginnings of an AT practice without even knowing it. Though few people have a dedicated AT practice, many people actually do bring a number of critical elements of this practice into their lives every day without being aware of it.

AT, it turns out, takes many forms, and different people tend to gravitate toward certain approaches. Your challenge is to experiment to find the one approach that resonates most or comes most easily to you. But there's a challenge in such a quest. The approach that may attract you the least and be the most challenging to cultivate may also be the one that yields the most profound impact. I've noticed this in my own practice, as well as the practice of too many others who ignore this ironic truth. Explore the approaches that come easiest to you, but also dance with the one or two that pose the greatest challenge. They may contain keys that unlock far bigger doors for you. Same thing with teachers and programs; find the ones that resonate with you most, rather than the ones your neighbor or office-mate is drawn to.

AT is among the most effective personal practices in steeling the creator against the fear and anxiety that ride along with the uncertainty of creation, but it's not the only daily mind-set force multiplier in our arsenal.

VISUALIZATION, VOODOO, AND THE CREATIVE MIND

For many years, visualization frustrated me. The typical instructions didn't work. Movies, books, blogs, and gurus tell you to create highly detailed pictures of outcomes, then see yourself already having achieved them. Slap pictures of a car, vacation, body, spouse, or dream house onto a vision board, then see, hear, smell, and feel yourself already enjoying them. Magically, the world rallies to deliver everything you want to your doorstep. If it doesn't work, it's because you haven't felt it deeply enough.

As an artist turned entrepreneur turned New York City lawyer turned back into entrepreneur turned yoga guy turned artist, I'm what I'd call a skeptical spiritualist. I'm open to everything, but I need to see it work in my own life to believe it. Even then, I'd feel a whole lot better if there was at least a wisp of nonbastardized science to hang my rational-brain hat on.

Beyond the fact that most pop-psych visualization focuses on the acquisition of material things and sidesteps the whole issue of the quest for deeper meaning (and a little requirement called insanely hard work over time), there's another thing that's always made it near impossible for me to follow the traditional directions, at least in the early phases of any quest.

When you're an artist or entrepreneur, it's rare that you can define the detailed ins and outs of your final creation with any level of accuracy before you begin it. You may have big ideas, plot lines, words, metaphors, inspirations, colors, light, energy, sound, markets to serve, ideas for products or services, or even prototypes to test. You may have identified the qualities, emotions, and experiences you hold dear and strive to create for others. But in the earliest stages you generally have very little idea what the final output is going to look like. Even if you do, it's very likely that if you're paying serious attention to your muse and your market, you will need to evolve that vision, often many times over, to become something radically different by the end of the process.

For the artist, entrepreneur, or other creator, the outcome-centric approach to visualization that's most commonly offered can be an exercise in both futility and frustration. Actually, it's worse. Because if you are someone who's capable of creating a highly specific definition of your precise outcome in advance and you follow the straightest line to that outcome and remain utterly committed to that vision, you'll get there faster. But you'll also increase the likelihood that the very same blinders that send you on a beeline toward your planned outcome will lead you to completely miss a host of unplanned paths and options that, had you been open to seeing them, would have markedly improved your final creation. You'll get exactly what you wanted, then realize it's not what it could have been.

In 1993, University of Hertfordshire professor and author of *The Luck Factor* (2004) Richard Wiseman conducted a fascinating experiment that demonstrated the potentially limiting impact of blind commitment to a goal and its connection to perceived good fortune and improved outcomes. As he reported in a 2003 article in the *Skeptical Inquirer,* Wiseman assembled two groups of individuals—one composed of people who considered themselves extremely lucky and one populated by those who considered themselves extremely unlucky. He then gave each group a newspaper and asked them to report the number of photographs inside. "On average, the unlucky people took about two minutes to count the photographs whereas the lucky people took just seconds," he wrote. "Why? Because the second page of the newspaper contained the message 'Stop counting – There are 43 photographs in this newspaper.' This message took up half of the page and was written in type that was over two inches high. It was staring everyone straight in the face, but the unlucky people tended to miss it and the lucky people tended to spot it."

Good fortune, it seems, smiles upon those who remain open to inviting possibilities and opportunities outside the rigid constructs of their immediate task, mission, or vision. Ones they would not and could not have foreseen. In any large-scale, long-term creative endeavor, the straightest line all too often leads not to the greatest possible outcome but rather to the most linear outcome, and leaves the potential to create genius on the table. There is often a great divide between creating exactly what you *sought* to create and creating what you were *capable* of creating.

When I think about what I want to create, I think about impact and qualities. I want to create a specific experience. I want to have a specific impact on people. I want to feel my heart pounding as often as I can, both when I create and when I think about how much the final creation resonates with me and with those who might enjoy or benefit from it.

I have ideas, strong ones, about where I want to go in the beginning, but whether it's a company, a book, or a painting, those ideas always evolve in profound, unseen, and unseeable ways between the time of conception and the moment of realization. How do you visualize that on day one? You can't. You may be able to fabricate scenarios where you feel the way you imagine you'll feel once you've created what you dream of creating. But the level of specificity required by popular visualization techniques just doesn't happen the way it's supposed to happen in the context of the long-term, large-scale creative endeavor.

If you're true to a process that provides for intelligent adaptation during the process of evolution, it can't. Even on the rare occasions when I've been able to fit my amorphous, quality/experience-driven vision into a square enough box to fit the generic instruction to define every detail of my desired outcome, I found it did nothing to guide my daily actions. It did zero to battle daily bursts of fear, uncertainty, and the resistance Steven Pressfield describes. Once you're further down the road, things become clearer. As you approach the constraint side of the creation spectrum and more and more elements take form, outcome visualization gets easier. But it's not a tool for the early days.

That's why, for years, I had so much trouble with the idea of visualization as a tool for accelerating movement toward any artistic or entrepreneurial vision or quest. Then, in 2007, a yoga student of mine, a woman who was pursuing her master's degree in applied positive psychology, shared some research she'd been doing on what really works and what doesn't in the world of visualization. She was exploring the science behind visualization to see if she could suss out what was voodoo and what had a real, verifiable basis in proof. She shared the research and opened my eyes to a completely novel approach to visualization that was built not around the quest of a long-term, easily defined vision, but on the need to take daily action in the context of any challenging endeavor.

The approach to visualization or mental simulation most often offered is something called outcome simulation. It asks you to create a vivid picture of a specific outcome as if it has already happened. Maybe it's crossing the finish line at a race, owning your dream house, toppling a government, getting an A on an exam, or doing your dream job for a living. Outcome simulation can be an effective tool. But for the reasons I've noted, for many artists, entrepreneurs, and even organizational teams charged with innovation, especially in the early days of creation, outcome is not the most powerful tool in the visualization arsenal.

There is, however, a different approach to visualization that has been shown in a number of published studies to be significantly more powerful than outcome visualization. It's also an approach that is custom-built for the daily mind-set of the long-term, large-scale creator, because it bolsters your ability to better define a project and take action on it on a daily basis. It's called process simulation, and true to its name, it focuses on visualizing not the outcome or goal but the steps and actions needed to get there.

In 1998 researchers Shelley E. Taylor, Lien B. Pham, Inna D. Rivkin, and David A. Armor published in *American Psychologist* the results of a study that tested the effectiveness of this approach. They divided eighty-four college students into three groups: a process simulation group, an outcome simulation, and a control group. Over a one-week period, for five minutes each day, students in the process-simulation group visualized the actions and steps needed to complete a specified project. At the same time, students in the outcome-simulation group visualized themselves having successfully completed the project. Students in a third control group did neither. The results were eye-opening:

- Compared to the control group, students in both the process and the outcome groups were more likely to begin the project on time. Both process and outcome simulation got people acting earlier than no simulation.
- The students who visualized themselves having successfully completed the project were significantly more likely to complete it on time.
- The students who visualized the steps needed to complete the project were more likely than both other groups to finish on time, and they generally considered the assignment easier than students in the other groups.

In a series of additional studies by Pham and Taylor on undergraduate students in 1997 and 1999, students who engaged in daily process simulation in anticipation of an exam started studying earlier than those who simply visualized getting an A. Not surprisingly, with more study, the process simulation group scored an average of eight points better on the exam than the outcome simulation group, who simply visualized getting an A.

The driving engine and greatest challenge in any long-term, creative endeavor is to act daily, especially in the face of great uncertainty, fear, risk, and anxiety. If you're working only in the mode of creation that closely aligns with your innate creation preference (insight or REP), this may not be a huge issue. But nearly every solo artist, entrepreneur, or other creator is charged with both parts of the process. As we've discussed, when you hit the part of the process that grates against you, it causes pain. You need all the help you can get to lean into it, get better at it, and move through it, because that's what it takes to create genius.

Outcome simulation or visualization is fairly useless as a tool to compel the gritty daily action needed for people like us, at least in the early days when uncertainty and learning necessarily rule the roost. Process simulation, as the research shows, fuels these daily actions. It drives you to carry out these daily steps and makes you more likely to start earlier, be more consistent, and experience these tasks as being less difficult.

Implementing Process Simulation

How do you make process simulation work for you? Emiliya Zhivotov-skaya, MAPP, offers three powerful ways to put this tool to work:

Define Your Daily Creation Ritual

We've talked about the power of certainty anchors and ritual, within the context of the creation process and in life. Some people are very aware of their rituals. They are a deliberate, tested, and applied part of their process. Others take a more haphazard approach. Process simulation can help define your daily creation rituals and actions.

Use It to Self-regulate or Stick to Your Ritual

Here's where this practice really shines. Actions and rituals have power when you do them. But then there's the side of the process that makes you want to hurl. Not always, but often enough to throw you off your game. Process visualization is another tool in the arsenal, because it allows you to visualize yourself doing the very things you need to do to move your creation forward.

If you're a writer, visualize yourself putting your notebook or pad in your bag, walking to your favorite café, choosing your table, ordering your favorite beverage, spending a few minutes reviewing handwritten notes, then opening your current creation and writing X words or for X minutes or hours, then taking a break to do Y, then coming back for your second creation about thirty minutes later. Visualize whatever works for you. Be true to the process, actions, and rituals that you can commit to.

Create a Tangible Manifestation of Your Commitment

While many people are strongly visual in their thought and learning, others are not. Asking those nonvisual people to visualize even small steps can be an exercise in futility, because their brains don't operate that way. Writing, however, can be a highly effective approach to process simulation. Rather than simply thinking and seeing the steps, rituals, and actions, take the extra step of writing them down. This changes the dynamic in a number of ways.

If you're visually oriented, it changes the medium and opens the process up to you in a way that would have been much more difficult, if not impossible, to accomplish if you simply kept it in your head. Creating a written manifestation of the steps also further ingrains them and provides a tangible prompt to spur action. Because when you write the steps down, you invariably see yourself doing them. So you're really just journaling your process simulation in real time.

To-do lists are perfect examples of this. Part of the reason they can be so effective (not always, for as we all know, they can be easily abused or used as crutches) is that they are effectively process simulation lists.

The time of day doesn't really matter—some people find it more effective to visualize and memorialize the following day's action steps the night before or the morning of.

Either way, the research is pretty clear: When you simulate taking the steps needed for creating your day, you end up taking those steps with greater regularity, moving through your creative process with greater ease, and becoming more likely not only to get to the end but to create on a higher level. You create momentum, and that is a powerful tool in the face of the undertow of uncertainty.

Which brings us to the next of our daily mind-set practices.

FOSTERING THE GROWTH MIND-SET

What if there were a switch you could flip that would enable you to look at challenge, struggle, judgment, and trial as sources of feedback, data points in the quest to get better at what you are striving for? That switch may not exist as such, but the groundbreaking work of Stanford professor Carol Dweck on mind-set and success is about as close as we can get.

In her book, *Mindset: The New Psychology of Success* (2006), she identifies what she calls the fixed and growth mind-sets. All of us, says Dweck, end up, through a blend of innate tendencies and environment, adopting one of two mind-sets: fixed or growth.

A person with a fixed mind-set assumes that success is based upon talent, not work. And they define talent as something that's not changeable. Through God or biology, you've got what you've got. When you hit the limits of that, it's game over. You can't perform better, create cooler stuff, write, paint, or build on a newer, higher level. The fixed mind-set is very common in music and the classic arts, where creative ability is often attributed to a "gift."

For a creator with a fixed mind-set, failing any test or being judged "not up to par" is a death knell because, in his mind, there's nothing he can do about it. Having to work at something is futile—you either have it or you don't. The result is that the moment you hit the edge of what comes easily and begin to get a taste of being judged as a non-prodigy, you back away. The opportunity for judgment starts to feel excruciating, and you begin to view the notion of trying to work through as a fatalistic effort that is doomed to fail. Why bother painting, writing, dancing, or striving to build an entrepreneurial venture, you ask, when the likelihood of being humiliated is so large and the opportunity to take your creation to the next level is essentially closed to you? You make excuses for not trying.

A person with a growth mind-set, on the other hand, assumes that work is the core driver of success and places less importance on genetics as a determining factor. When met with a test or an opportunity to be judged, she is far more likely to view it as yet another opportunity to learn what her current state of knowledge and ability is, then use that information to guide and even motivate her work toward the next level. For the person with a growth mind-set, instances of judgment, evaluation, or testing, whether public or private, may not always feel good, but they're an important part of being able to get better faster and succeed bigger. Such people not only endure judgment but often invite it.

Criticism has value because there's something you can do about it. The more any creator can cultivate the growth mind-set, the less important judgment-leveling changes in environment become, because such a person has already developed the ability to lean into judgment and incorporate it as necessary data for higher-level creation and success.

When I was first exposed to Dweck's work, I freaked out—and not just because it resonated so strongly. I started thinking about my own process, about whether I'd cultivated a growth or a fixed mind-set. It turns out that I lean pretty strongly toward the growth side of the spectrum. Not always, but I'm a big believer in work as the source of most genius, along with a sprinkling of genetic pixie dust.

Then I turned my attention to my daughter and started wondering about her. I reviewed how, according to Dweck, the language a parent uses in praising, engaging with, and correcting a child can play a substantial role in fostering one or the other mind-set, regardless of the child's organic starting point. I started catching myself saying things like, "Oh, sweety, that painting is so beautiful. You're so talented." Or, "Great job on that math test. You've got a real gift for numbers."

Such comments sound innocuous enough on the surface, but they are textbook examples of unintentionally programming your kids to adopt a fixed mind-set, capping their perceived ability to learn beyond what comes easily by attributing success, performance, and mastery to a perceived talent or gift and by implicitly discrediting work as the primary source of growth, mastery, and success.

I began to change the language I use with my daughter. Instead of focusing on talent and ability, I now say things like, "I'm so proud of how hard you worked on X." I focus less on the outcome and more on the process, framing tests, trials, or contests as opportunities to see where you're at and to learn how to use them to inform your work going forward. Just as the language we use when we speak to people we influence plays a role in how we cultivate one or the other mind-set, the language we use and the expectations we set with ourselves are critical.

Cultivation of a growth mind-set starts with an understanding that greatness is largely about work. There may be a genetic element, which more often is on the exclusionary rather than the greatness side. But the far larger part of genius lies in understanding that not talent but doing the work is the core driver of greatness. This understanding frees us to lean into the uncertainty, accept risk, and seek judgment with the understanding that, offered constructively, those actions are what will move us closer to our ability to create what we're here to create.

So far, the daily mind-set practices we've explored have been largely based in activities that directly train our brain and thoughts. But there's one last daily practice that may well be our greatest ally.

THE CREATIVE BRAIN ON EXERCISE

For more than thirty years, Haruki Murakami has dazzled the world with his beautifully crafted words, most often in the form of novels and short stories. But his book *What I Talk About When I Talk About Running* (2008) opens a rare window into his life and process, revealing an obsession with running and how it fuels his creative process.

An excerpt from a 2004 interview with Murakami in *The Paris Review* brings home the connection between physical strength and creating extraordinary work:

> When I'm in writing mode for a novel, I get up at 4:00 A.M. and work for five to six hours. In the afternoon, I run for ten kilometers or swim for fifteen hundred meters (or do both), then I read a bit, and listen to some music. I go to bed at 9:00 P.M. I keep to this routine every day without variation. The repetition itself becomes the important thing; it's a form of mesmerism. I mesmerize myself to reach a deeper state of mind. But to hold to such repetition for so long—six months to a year—requires a good amount of mental and physical strength. In that sense, writing a long novel is like survival training. Physical strength is as necessary as artistic sensitivity.

Murakami is guided by what the great scholars, writers, thinkers, and creators of ancient Greece knew yet so many modern-day creators have abandoned.

The physical state of our bodies can either serve or subvert the quest to create genius. We all know this intuitively. But with rare exceptions, because life seems to value output over the humanity of the process and the ability to sustain genius, attention to health, fitness, and exercise almost always takes a backseat. That's tragic. Choosing art over health rather than art fueled by health kills you faster; it also makes the process so much more miserable and leads to poorer, slower, less innovative, and shallower creative output.

As Dr. John Ratey noted in his seminal work *Spark: The Revolutionary New Science of Exercise and the Brain* (2008), exercise isn't just about physical health and appearance. It also has a profound effect on your brain chemistry, physiology, and neuroplasticity (the ability of the brain to literally rewire itself). It affects not only your ability to think, create, and solve, but your mood and ability to lean into uncertainty, risk, judgment, and anxiety in a substantial, measurable way, even though until very recently it's been consistently cast out as the therapeutic bastard child in lists of commonly accepted treatments for anxiety and depression.

In 2004 the esteemed *New England Journal of Medicine* (NEJM) published a review of treatments for generalized anxiety disorder that noted thirteen pharmaceuticals, each with a laundry list of side effects, but nothing about exercise. In response, *NEJM* published a letter by renowned cardiologists Richard Milani and Carl Lavie, who had written more than seventy papers on the effect of exercise on the heart, eleven of them focused on anxiety. That letter criticizes the original article for omitting exercise, which, the writers note, "has been shown to lead to reductions of more than 50 percent in the prevalence of the symptoms of anxiety. This supports exercise training as an additional method to reduce chronic anxiety."

Ratey details many data points on the connection between exercise and mind-set; among them the following:

- A 2004 study led by Joshua Broman-Fulks of the University of Southern Mississippi that showed students who walked at 50 percent of their maximum heart rates or ran on treadmills at 60 to 90 percent of their maximum heart rates reduced their sensitivity to anxiety, and that rigorous exercise worked better. "Only the high-intensity group felt less afraid of the physical symptoms of anxiety, and the distinction started to show up after just the second exercise session."

- A 2006 Dutch study of 19,288 twins and their families that demonstrated that those who exercised were "less anxious, less depressed, less neurotic, and also more socially outgoing."

- A 1999 Finnish study of 3,403 people that revealed that those who exercised two to three times a week "experience significantly less depression, anger, stress, and 'cynical distrust.'"

Ratey points to a number of proven chemical pathways, along with the brain's neuroplastic abilities, as the basis for these changes, arguing that exercise changes the expression of fear and anxiety, as well as the way the brain processes them from the inside out.

Studies now prove that aerobic exercise both increases the size of the prefrontal cortex and facilitates interaction between it and the amygdala. This is vitally important to creators because the prefrontal cortex, as we discussed earlier, is the part of the brain that helps tamp down the amygdala's fear and anxiety signals.

For artists, entrepreneurs, and any other driven creators, exercise is a powerful tool in the quest to help transform the persistent uncertainty, fear, and anxiety that accompany the quest to create from a source of suffering into something less toxic, then potentially even into fuel.

This is not to suggest that anyone suffering from a generalized or trait (that is, long-term) anxiety disorder avoid professional help and self-treat with exercise alone. People who suffer from anxiety should not hesitate to seek out the guidance of a qualified mental health-care professional.

The point is to apply the lessons from a growing body of research on the therapeutic effect of exercise on anxiety, mood, and fear to the often sustained low-level anxiety that rides organically along with the uncertainty of creation. Anyone involved in a creative endeavor should tap exercise as a potent elixir to help transform the uncomfortable sensation of anxiety from a source of pain and paralysis into something not only manageable but harnessable.

Exercise, it turns out, especially at higher levels of intensity, is an incredibly potent tool in the quest to train in the arts of the fear alchemist.

Exercise Accelerates Genius

Until now, we've been talking about exercise largely as a salve for the uncomfortable side of the creation process. But its impact is felt way beyond the removal of pain. Just as AT does, exercise serves as a catalyst for improving brain function, problem solving, decision making, and creativity. Done on a regular, routine, ritualized basis, it also serves as yet another highly effective certainty anchor.

A substantial body of research now connects exercise to improvements in mood. Another set of studies connects improved mood to creativity and productivity. Given the number of moody, disgruntled, yet productive, successful, and critically acclaimed artists and entrepreneurs in the world, you'd be inclined to doubt the conclusions. But the data is solid, which tends to make you wonder how much better some creative bodies of work might have been and how much more work might have been created by the typical angst-ridden creators had they been shaking their booties instead of their fists.

In a 2002 study, Rhode Island College professor Stephen Ramocki found a significant relationship between vigorous aerobic exercise and creativity, including an increase in creativity immediately following exercise. In a more recent study published in *Creativity Research Journal* in 2005, Ramocki's colleague David Blanchette sought to find out (a) whether even moderate exercise had a similar effect and (b) whether the increase in creativity would extend beyond the period of time immediately following exercise. The answer to both is yes. While higher-intensity exercise seems to be more effective in countering anxiety and elevating mood, Blanchette found that even moderate exercise yielded a significant increase in creativity that was still present two hours after the exercise was completed.

Broadening out in a quest to better understand how exercise interacts with cognitive ability, a 2005 study of 210 workers by Professor Jim McKenna at Leeds Metropolitan University revealed that on the day employees exercise, their mood as well as their work performance were substantially improved, as measured by their ability to manage their time, increase output, and improve mental and interpersonal performance. And an October 2007 *Newsweek* article reporting on a series of studies by Professor Arthur Kramer, a psychologist at the University of Illinois, showed that daily aerobic exercise can actually grow new brain cells, especially in the hippocampus, the area that controls memory and learning, and in the frontal lobes, which are chiefly responsible for executive function—planning, abstract thinking, decision making and adaptation, processing sensory information, taking constructive action, not taking destructive action, and knowing the difference between the two. Exercise fostered improved performance on psychological tests of the subjects' ability to answer questions more quickly and accurately. The research also seems to show there is a "use it or lose it" effect once you are well into adulthood. Stop exercising and the increases quickly fade.

Beyond the research, you need only to look at the occupants of many of the top executive suites for a demonstration of the critically important contribution of exercise to professional achievement. Those who aspire to professional greatness hold their daily workout sacred, and those seeking to hold on to their seats at the table view movement not just as a way to look and feel better, but as a mission-critical creation tool.

Still, a large number of artists and entrepreneurs resist exercise as a key element in their ability to do what they most want to do—make cool stuff that speaks to a lot of people. In the case of artists, I often wonder if that resistance is born of a cultural chasm that many artists grew up with, where jocks were jocks, artists were artists, hackers were hackers, and never the twain would meet. For more sedentary solo creators, historical assumptions about who exercises and who doesn't can impose some very real limits on a behavior that would be very beneficial on so many levels.

On the entrepreneur side, the excuse I've heard (and used myself) over and over is "I'm launching a damn company and my hair's on fire. I don't have time to work out." The sad truth is that if we make the time to exercise, it makes us so much more productive and leads to such improved creativity, cognitive function, and mood that the time we need for doing it will open up and then some—making us so much happier and better at the art of creation, to boot.

How to Make Exercise Fun Again

When you were a child, you ran around all day, played catch, climbed trees, swam, danced around, jumped rope, hopscotched, and bounced off walls until you passed out. Back then, you called it play and you loved it. But now you call it exercise and you loathe it. Indeed, every time you think about working out, your entire body forms the word "Ugh!" What changed?

What most people don't realize is that it's not the work part of exercise they hate—it's the boredom. Somewhere in your journey from child to adult, you went from mind-engaging, ever-changing, attention-demanding activities to mind-numbing, repetitive movement. From kick the can to the treadmill. From dancing around to the stepper. From play to exercise. Why?

Because as life becomes fuller and schedules get tighter, you turn to the seemingly easiest, most efficient option to satisfy your fitness needs. This inevitably leads you to the steps of the nearest gym. Most facilities allocate the largest portions of their floor space and budget to legions of treadmills, rowers, steppers, weight, and repetitive-motion machines. When a person makes a dogged commitment, this approach to exercise works. The problem is that for most people indoor, repetition-driven, machine-based exercise is relentlessly dull. It pushes people to hate something that, approached differently, they might love.

The industry knows this and has responded primarily by positioning televisions, radios, Web terminals, and computers around the workout space to distract you from the fact that the options being offered, while efficient, are astoundingly devoid of joy. These headphone-driven entertainment systems also have the inadvertent effect of killing human interaction and, along with it, community, a key determinant of long-term participation. The net effect is large-scale dropout. A strong aversion to exercise in the format offered by many gyms leads many to dispense with a part of life that, approached differently, would be a source of great joy.

Granted, there are exceptions and, thankfully, the number is growing, but this phenomenon is a significant part of the reason why some 90 percent of U.S. adults readily admit to needing to exercise to stay healthy and pain- and disease-free, while only about 15 percent actually join or remain members of health clubs.

If you want to love exercise again, you need to shift your mind-set away from the pure "physical efficiency" model and back to the mind-engaging ambrosia of play and community. Indeed, the demand for varied, community-driven exercise has begun to fuel an explosion in alternative forms of movement and exercise experiences and settings among adults. These activities—think martial arts, CrossFit, boot-camps, obstacle challenges, modified indoor cycling, P90X, power yoga, dancing, team sports, boxing, badminton, rock climbing—engage the mind, cultivate passion, and inspire joy.

How do you apply this understanding to your own fitness quest?

First, shift your focus away from minutes, miles per hour, repe-titions, and calories. Figure out your motion profile—what makes you tick, what jazzes you from a movement standpoint. Then build on this to find or create the most mind-engaging and downright "exhila-rating" workouts of your life. Find things that (a) require you to pay intense attention, that change constantly and challenge your mental as well as your physical abilities and (b) are community driven.

Remember what you loved to do as a child. Think about all the great options available to kids today. When it comes to exercise, your psychological need for engagement is no different now than when you were a kid. With the added stresses of adulthood, your need for ac-tivities that not only get you healthy but clear your mind is even greater. It's a bit odd to say, but you need to regress to progress. Once you have found your activities, you can do them alone or with a part-ner or a group. You can do them at home or at a facility, whichever works best for you.

But does it really work? Will this mind-engaging movement be as effective as your typical repetition/distraction exercise? With rare ex-ceptions, yes, and even more so. There may be more traditional or "scientific" ways to exercise that are more effective at burning calories or building strength in a perfect world. But if you hate them so much that after two months you quit and go back to lying on your couch, those super-efficient exercises end up being no more effective than a tub of wings, a bucket of bonbons, and an easy chair.

Think about it:

- Option 1: Attempt to run for thirty minutes on a treadmill every day, plugged into a terminal or TV, avoiding human contact. Hate it so much that after six weeks you quit, never to return to the gym.
- Option 2: Dance/play for thirty minutes a day for six weeks in a mind-engaging, supportive, community-driven environment. Then bump it up to forty-five minutes because you are having so much fun. Continue indefinitely.

Shift your focus from what works in a controlled, "test tube" environment to what works in the real world. If you're one of the small percentage of people who are genuinely drawn to lifting weights and using machines based on repetition and distraction, by all means have at it. You're one of the lucky few. If not, cast a wider net to explore not only what, on paper, burns the most calories or builds the most muscle, but what makes exercise so enjoyable, engaging, and fulfilling that you will do whatever it takes to add more to your life every day. You need to find a way to feel good *about* exercising and to feel good *while* exercising.

A Word of Caution

Exercise is clearly one of the most effective tools in the trained fear alchemist and creator's arsenal. Some of the benefits come fairly immediately, and at lower levels of intensity. Others require higher levels of intensity over a longer period of time.

One of the biggest mistakes people make when they begin to exercise is going too hard, too fast. Don't do it. It can be dangerous, causing illness, injury, or worse. If you've been sedentary for a while, be sure to talk to your qualified health-care provider before beginning any new exercise program. If at all possible, seek out face-to-face instruction for safety and intelligence and small groups for camaraderie and accountability.

PUTTING IT TOGETHER

Changes in environment, culture, and the people who guide and inform your creation process can make a tremendous difference in the way you experience the journey. But at some point, you need to stop looking for solutions outside yourself and turn your attention inward. Cultivating a daily personal practice helps steel you against the fear and anxiety that come from embracing uncertainty, risk, and exposure to judgment. It also significantly ramps up your cognitive function, ability to come up with ideas, and general state of mind, and helps foster a sense of equanimity in the face of what is at times a raging creation storm.

Exercise and AT, individually, are extraordinary creation force multipliers. Together, they are capable of transforming not only what you're capable of bringing to life, but how you experience the process of creation.

There are several things you should focus on as you move forward.

Building Your AT Practice

Start with the three fundamental approaches shared in this chapter. Explore them and see what feels right to you.

- For more information on easily accessible approaches to AT and to download complementary guided meditations in mp3 format, visit JonathanFields.com/mindset.
- For moving AT: Look for activities that either require intense at-

tention or are rhythmic and safe enough to allow you to focus on the rhythm. If you find yourself limited to indoor, repetition-based exercises because of safety, suitability, or environmental issues, these activities can become deeply contemplative and energizing experiences.

Shifting to a Growth Mind-Set

Professor Carol Dweck is the leading authority on understanding the differences between fixed and growth mind-sets and, if needed, cultivating a shift from the former to the latter. Read her book *Mindset: The New Psychology of Success* for detailed information about how to undertake the change.

Exploring Both Outcome and Process Visualization

Explore the suggestions provided above for building process simulation into your daily routine and your creation processes. If you're strongly nonvisual, pay special attention to the advice about integrating to-do lists with process simulation.

Discovering Your Exercise M.O. and Committing to Regular Participation

Exercise is one of the few activities on the planet that just about everyone agrees is important, yet the overall participation is abysmal. Even beyond general health, vitality, and disease prevention, a mountain of research also positions exercise at the center of your ability to create and perform at the highest levels professionally. Two strong bits of advice.

First, read Dr. John Ratey's book *Spark: The Revolutionary New Science of Exercise and the Brain*. It will open your eyes to the importance of exercise in every aspect of your life as nothing you've read before has done. It will clarify the role exercise plays in preserving and even bolstering your ability to lean into uncertainty, fear, and anxiety as you strive to build something extraordinary.

Then begin to explore ways to move your body, starting gently, preferably under the guidance of a professional, and with the support of a community that's rooting for your success. Do not limit yourself to traditional, repetition- and distraction-based options. Focus not only on effectiveness, but also on joy, engagement, and community.

8

SEE THE FOREST

WE'VE EXPLORED THE power of shifting your environment and creative culture, dropping certainty anchors, tapping technology, and cultivating a daily mind-set and physical practice. All of these tactics will help you to embrace uncertainty, risk, and exposure on the level that fuels extraordinary outcomes. But there are still some bigger issues we need to address, ones that have a profound impact on your ability to stay sane through the creative process. We need to take a step back and revisit how you're doing as you execute on your vision, as well as why you are pushing forward, what your creation journey is doing to and for your life, and even whether you should keep going. It's time to zoom out, to explore the forest beyond the trees a bit more fully.

In this chapter, we'll explore the driving role of a calling to create. We'll address the often brutally hard question of when to soldier on and when to walk away. And we'll take a hard look at the potentially destructive impact many all-consuming creative quests have on life beyond the endeavor and how that can filter back into the work to either inspire or derail it.

CALLED TO CREATE

"You do the thing you can't not do."

I first heard the phrase when researching my earlier book. I was talking to Gina Trapani, a tech writer, coder, and Lifehacker.com founding editor. I asked why she'd left her job in 2005 to start Life hacker.com. She gave a number of reasons but in the end pointed to the phrase above. Beyond the litany of traditional reasons and rationales, it came down to something deeper, something not so easily defined but ever so strongly felt.

Peter Wallace, the Brooklyn Artists Gym founder who's on a quest to sculpt a massive wave sculpture, cited the same phrase. Not every creative endeavor rises to the level of work you "can't not do," work you're being called to. But when it does, you cannot underestimate the power of the commitment that attaches to it and the tireless action it inspires.

Trapani's words, with subtle variation, appeared as I began to zoom my lens out to explore what drives people to create, to build or start movements, be they solo artists, entrepreneurs, or leaders of large organizations. Why did you start that company? Why do you paint? Why do you write books, music, or poems? Why did you choose coding over med school? Why did you make that movie? Why is all of your work so dark? What's kept you going this long? What stops you from quitting?

Over and over, I got some variation of the same answer: "It's not just what I do; it's why I'm here."

There's magic behind a creative process driven not by a mandate from someone else or a passing interest, but by a sense of a calling or deeper purpose. When Steve Jobs and Steve Wozniak launched what would become Apple, it wasn't out of a desire to just do a job or project or make some money. It was about doing what nobody'd ever done before. It was about making insanely cool things, starting a revolution, changing the world. When you talk to most actors, writers, or painters, they don't do it because they thought it'd be a good way to make a buck. Turns out it's a relatively brutal way to make a buck. They do it because it's the thing they can't not do. They are being pulled into it by something that's often not quite definable, but that nevertheless exerts a certain gravity that's near impossible to resist.

Kris Carr is an extraordinary example. On Valentine's Day in 2003, at the age of thirty-one, she was diagnosed with a very rare form of cancer that had already progressed to stage 4 and spread to her liver and lungs. Her first doctor recommended removing the organs and waiting for a transplant, which seemed a horrifying course of treatment to Carr, one she ultimately refused to accept. She set out on a mission to reclaim her health and to find the best doctor in the world for this extraordinarily rare disease. She found him in Boston, and though his practice was closed, she convinced him to take her on as a patient. They began to work together, and early on he told her that her cancer was very slow growing; he recommended that she go out and live life as fully as possible.

The experience created a different frame, a new story line for her life. Until then, she'd been an actress for pretty much her entire working life, but she had always had a jones to get behind the camera—to be the one telling the stories. This was her moment. She had nothing to lose. So in addition to radically changing her lifestyle and nutrition in a quest to become as healthy as possible, she set out to create a documentary about her journey called *Crazy, Sexy Cancer*. She wanted to tell a story about not lying down and waiting for death, about rising up and living not under but beyond the shadow of one of the scariest words on the planet.

Everyone around her thought she was nuts. Nobody would want to see a movie about cancer, let alone buy or show it. And the title, sexy and cancer together? With her condition, she was told, she shouldn't be doing things that would cause her so much stress. But Carr didn't listen. She couldn't. This was the thing she couldn't not do. Her calling came from a death sentence that had given her permission to live. Damned if anyone else was going to take that away from her.

Crazy, Sexy Cancer premiered at the South by Southwest film festival in 2007 to rave reviews and was soon after sold to the cable network TLC, where it drew a huge audience and launched a movement that continues to this day. An evangelist for plant-based nutrition and living fully, Carr's third book, *Crazy Sexy Diet* (2011), became a *New York Times* best seller, and she's now working on her fourth book and speaks globally to those with cancer and anyone open to living a better life. Through all of this, her cancer has not only slowed but stopped growing. Still it remains her teacher—guiding her calling, her creations, and her life.

When you are called to create, the psychology of the endeavor also changes. Experiencing a calling creates a sense of deeper conviction, of purpose that often you, even as the creator or vision leader, don't fully understand. It's not religious, though it can be, but there is a sense that "in this moment, this is what I must do." Amorphous as the source of the drive may be, this sense of deep commitment changes how you experience the emotions and challenges of the process. It helps steel you against the demons that dance around in your head, the resistance that taunts and teases you away from your work. It fortifies your uncertainty scaffolding, giving more ability to lean into risk and exposure, to act when you're being judged from all sides. Judgment be damned, you're doing what you're here to do.

When you are driven by a calling or a deeply personal quest and you allow that calling to inspire action, you live in the world differently. You do a thousand little things you've never done before. You act and interact with more confidence and vitality. Your personal energy changes. The way you speak, the way you carry yourself, your willingness to move heaven and earth and to share and evangelize your vision become palpable manifestations of your will to succeed. You begin to radiate the quest. You come alive. And people around you not only feel it, but become drawn to it. And to you.

As Guy Kawasaki explains in his book *Enchantment* (2011), purpose and passion enchant people. They want to be around you. They want to help you. They want to rally to your cause—just as Virgin America, Sony, and an army of film, sound, editing, and production experts rallied to Erik Proulx's quest to create his first documentary when he announced to the world his commitment to do the thing that he couldn't not do.

You may have experienced the power of being called to create, either as the visionary or the one captivated by someone else's vision. It may well have been more compelling than any well-constructed argument for action. But in the end, such a calling is often based on a blend of unyielding faith and deep conviction that "this must be done." Nothing more, nothing less. And on the backs of that hard-to-defend faith and conviction lie some of the greatest creations and careers the world has seen.

Which leads us to our second big-picture exploration. Whether you're called to create or even when, as happens far more often, you are driven by some lesser, though compelling, reason, how do you know when to keep moving forward or to call it a day?

KNOWING WHEN TO HOLD AND WHEN TO FOLD

"I feel amazing," said the voice at the other end of the phone. "It's like that tightness in my stomach is gone. I can breathe again. And I slept like a baby for the first time in months."

"Really?" I replied. "What gives?"

"Well . . . I've decided to pull the plug on the business, and the moment I did, everything got better. I wasn't anxious anymore, I felt like a weight had been lifted. Like after struggling and working like crazy for months, I finally got my peace of mind, my life back. I feel totally free again. Unencumbered."

The voice belonged to a client, Anne. It was a call I'd taken before from many people and in many different variations. After six months of planning, hundreds of hours of preparation, site building, design, asset creation, product development, copywriting, casting, filming, editing, system testing, and marketing prep, she'd launched a new business. The plan was to grow it aggressively over the following two years until it was successful enough to support her.

"So," I asked, "do you trust me?"

"Implicitly. Why?"

"Because I'm about to ask you something that's going to make you angry at me. And very likely kill your 'free as a bird' buzz. I need to know whether walking away from this venture was genuinely a good call or whether it was born out of your inability to handle the uncertainty, the exposure, and the risk that rides along with the birthing of any deeply meaningful creative endeavor. Put another way, we need to figure out whether you're confusing genuine peace of mind with the passing lack of angst that follows the demise of a dream but precedes a mounting wave of regret."

"Oh."

"I want you to close your eyes and visualize something. Imagine, just for the moment, that you didn't make the call to shut down the business. Yeah, I know, you've made your decision. You feel really good about it. Just humor me.

"Now place yourself forward in time. It's two years from today. Everything you dreamed of making happen in your business has happened. You've succeeded beyond your wildest imagination. Every goal has been met, every team formed, every product and service launched and embraced, a vibrant culture grown. You're earning enough to live well in the world, impacting people on a deep, meaningful level and building a real legacy. Maybe you don't have precise clarity about any of those things; that's not unusual. So think about the experiences you want to create, both in your life and in others.

"See it, feel it, hear it, smell it, taste it . . . drink it in.

"Okay, now answer me these two questions . . . One, where are you feeling it? Does it stop in your mind, or are you feeling it in your whole body? Your heart, your chest, your gut?

"Everywhere," she said. "I can barely breathe."

"Okay. Second question. That scenario I just laid out, do you still want it?"

Silence. Thirty seconds go by.

"Yes. I'd kill for it."

That moment changed everything. It was an end transformed into a beginning. Her willingness to sit with the discomfort of not knowing how it would end was the difference between a future that continued a joyless decline into the void and an entirely new direction defined by substantially more creativity, fulfillment, freedom, and, yes, money.

Moments like this happen all the time in every creative process, when we ask some variation of the following:

- Is this project, idea, or quest still worth pursuing? Do I need to either shut it down or go about it in a radically different way?
- Is what I'm feeling just resistance, the lizard brain, anxiety, and fear that needs to be leaned into, or is it the accumulation of enough experience and data to tell me the smart move is to move on?

I've come face-to-face with these two questions countless times as a writer, an entrepreneur, a painter, a musician, and even a lawyer. On a more immediate level, the questions relate to the project you're working on. If you're a painter creating a collection of work, you may start to feel the questions arise as you explore whether a canvas or the collection is taking shape as you have envisioned it. On a more expansive level, the question emerges in the context of whether you should even be a painter or a writer, a coder, an entrepreneur, a CEO. I've seen actors struggle to build careers for decades, never coming close to earning enough to cover their bills. Yet they keep on keeping on, because their big break could be one audition away. And this is what they feel called to do.

These are some of the most difficult and defining moments every creator faces. I've been told by legendary entrepreneurs, "If you have to ask, assume it's resistance and soldier on." They claim that you just know whether or not a project is meant to be. But I've witnessed countless people commit to perpetually unsuccessful projects or careers or, on the other side of the spectrum, come a breath away from what would've been breakthrough success had they just held on a bit longer.

So I began to explore a more systematic process, a set of benchmarks, tests, and questions that might better guide these moments and help people decide whether to keep leaning into the journey, alter their course, or walk away and do something entirely different.

We start by asking, "What was your inciting motivation?" What made you undertake this endeavor to begin with. Was it, in some form, the expression of a calling? Was it something to keep you busy? Was it about serving a group of people, solving a problem, or serving up a delight? Was it about money or doing anything you could to get your parents off your back and avoid grad school? Begin by going back to the time surrounding your decision to create whatever it is you're creating and answer this question. Then move on to the next question.

In light of the information and experiences you've had along the journey to date, does that original motive still hold true? Are you still equally or even more determined to make it happen? And given what you now know, do you believe you can make it happen?

In his book *Getting to Plan B*, Randy Komisar suggests setting up what he calls a dashboard. You create a grid that identifies all of your major data points, assumptions, and leaps of faith on day one, then revisit it at regular intervals to assess what remains valid. Komisar's system helps identify at a sooner point when your initial plan may be starting to go off the rails and gives you an objective set of data to help decide what your next move should be. For entrepreneurs, especially in start-up phases, it's a great tool to help answer the big questions and decide whether, as more data comes in, to hold, change your hand, or fold.

But I've also found that these decisions can't be made entirely on data. It's also important, especially for solo creators and bootstrap entrepreneurs, to add a more subjective exploration to the process—one that dives deeper into whether, data aside, there are other reasons to consider soldiering on, adapting, or jumping ship.

The following additional questions will help you go one level deeper and will prompt you to explore what's really happening in these critical moments. They'll help you understand, on a level that adds clarity to the decision, whether you're reacting to an inability to handle fear and uncertainty or to real data and constructive intuition that's telling you to stop.

- Is this something you can't not do, regardless of whether you ever earn enough to live well in the world doing it?
- Are you more connected to the medium and your solution or your desire to serve a market?
- If you believe in your heart that what you set out to accomplish is highly likely to happen in the full glory you first imagined, would you still want that result?
- Would the data or feedback you've gathered to date require you to change the endeavor in such a substantial way that, while it may be more likely to succeed, the final creation, process, or

career will no longer satisfy the needs and desires that drew you into the quest to start with?

That last question is big, especially for entrepreneurs. It's not unusual to begin an endeavor with a strong sense of what you'd like to offer and whom you'd like to serve, only to have your market eventually tell you that you've missed the mark. For many entrepreneurs and creators, that's not a death knell. It's just a signpost that it's time to pivot the model, the solution, or even the culture and vision.

Behance CEO Scott Belsky's Action Method products are designed to help make creative professionals more productive. They work exceptionally well. If any given product they bring to market bombs, it'll hurt, but it's not game over. The entrepreneur just needs to figure out how to better serve the market with the next round of solutions. Belsky's vision is not to create the current line of Action Method products, but rather to create tools and processes that make creatives more productive. What those look like will change over time. And that allegiance to a market, rather than a specific product, gives him a lot of leeway to continue to test, build, bomb, and evolve.

All too often, that's not how start-ups or even established product-development teams operate. They are wedded more to their particular solution than to the notion of serving a market. When they start to have problems with that product, ones that aren't fixable with easy tweaks, they have a very difficult time moving through these moments.

Without a willingness to pivot your solution and model, the endeavor is likely to come to an end. One of the big lessons for entrepreneurs and solution-development teams is to think very seriously about the inciting motivation for their endeavors. Is the vision connected to a single product or the desire to serve a market? The latter is far more likely to set in motion a quest that is sustainable, especially if the market evolves over time. Which sends us squarely back to that final question: Even if you could adapt and move forward, should you?

It's one thing to evolve your quest in response to new data in an effort to create something that's better aligned with what your market needs and wants. But it's also important, at that moment, to ask whether that pivot will so substantially change the nature of the endeavor that it makes you no longer as intimately connected with it.

If evolving to meet your market means stripping away the things that drew you to the quest in the first place, you'll end up on track to create something everyone else loves . . . except you. And that will eventually cannibalize your soul. You'll end up hating what you do every day and looking for ways to get out, even if what you've created appears to be outwardly successful.

This happens all the time, in business and in art. Many actors are drawn to the craft because of the opportunity to tell stories, illuminate the human condition, and stir souls. But somewhere along the line, compelling stories and gravitas give way to a stable, yet incrementally less-fulfilling reputation as the perfect actor for consumer goods commercials. The market is telling you, "That's where we want you," so because you have bills to pay, that's what you do. You've found a way to make the business of acting work, but the way you're doing it is gutting you. You're outwardly successful in your chosen field, but inwardly empty.

You have a choice to make: You can either keep doing what you were called to do, but in a way that no longer honors the call and fills you up. You can work like crazy to redefine the box you've built and potentially try all manner of unconventional approaches to making what you want to do work. Or you can surrender to the notion that to act in the roles that honor your calling, you'll have to spend the better part of your life earning the bulk of your living some other way and be okay with that.

These are all tough decisions. These questions can be incredibly helpful in sussing out whether what you're feeling is just fear and uncertainty or a failure of your initial assumptions that will require you to either change how you're pursuing your quest or end it.

While the conversation in this chapter has focused around the decision to hold, adapt, or fold, there is one other phenomenon that often occurs in the lives of creators that poses an even greater challenge: the inability to pull yourself out of your quest.

CREATIVE ADDICTION AND THE MYTH OF BALANCE

In a post to my blog on May 2010, I shared a quote on the creative mind from Pearl S. Buck that ended, "without the creating of music or poetry or books or buildings or something of meaning, his very breath is cut off from him. He must create, must pour out creation. By some strange, unknown, inward urgency he is not really alive unless he is creating."

Then I asked my tribe:

- Is this true?
- If so, is the creative process an addiction?
- If it is, is that a good thing, a bad thing . . . or just a thing?

From this brief quote and three simple questions, a long debate ensued in the comments. Around the time I published Buck's quote, I also had a chance to sit down with Robert McKee, one of the world's foremost authorities on the structure of storytelling. Through his international Story seminars and a book of the same name, McKee has trained tens of thousands of screenwriters, television writers, and authors, including a laundry list of people who've won every award possible. I had just taken his four-day seminar in New York Ctiy in which he shared his belief that, with rare exceptions, it takes years, if not decades, of full-time devotion to develop your writing and story-telling craft. For every page that's good enough to keep, he said, you need to throw away ten. If he's right, to get a decent 400-page novel, you'd need to write 4,000 pages.

Those numbers are a bit jarring, though in my experience they're completely on the mark. McKee's calculation also jibes with the 10,000-hour rule popularized by Malcolm Gladwell in *Outliers* (2008), which argues that greatness in nearly any field is not about talent, but rather the accumulation of a bare minimum of 10,000 hours of deliberate practice. That often takes between ten and twenty years for even the most devout practitioner.

In a January 2011 post on her blog, Y Combinator co-founder Jessica Livingston came at the issue from the standpoint of start-up entrepreneurship:

> Startups are a huge amount of work. If you have a successful startup, you will most likely need to give up many of the "softer" things in life. You won't be able to date as much. You won't take long vacations. You might find yourself working almost every day of the year. Your family and friends will complain that they never see you.
>
> Even if you don't mean to blow everything off, you will become so consumed with your startup that it will occupy most of your waking thoughts. . . . Paul Graham always said having a successful startup is like condensing 40 years of working into 4 extremely stressful ones. This deal just isn't for everyone.

Which begs the question: What kind of insane, drug-induced obsession do you need to have to spend that much time madly pursuing the quest to build something from nothing? Do you really *have* to go to that place to succeed? If so, is there a way to stake your claim but still have a life?

If you talk to most traditional artists and entrepreneurs, and they're being honest, many will share their own variation of Buck's observations and Livingston's blog post, revealing a compulsion that, in many of its traits, seems to rise to the level of addiction, in part because they love what they do so much they start to feel empty when they're not doing it. Others, who are very driven to get "there" and who know that getting there almost always takes a long, intense effort, calculate that the more they work, the faster they'll get to a place of mastery, genius, respect.

There is some truth to this. But there's also a very dark underbelly. The lure of creative-obsessive behavior pulls you toward a single vehicle of creative output but ends up pushing you away from everything and everyone else in your life. Connections you once had to people and activities, even those you claim are the most important things in your universe, wither and eventually die of neglect. Stepping out of your something-from-nothing bubble turns into pain, so you stay in, where you know your trusted muse will always arrive at some point to offer up the next hit. It becomes a "chicken and egg" thing fairly quickly.

Was it the bad relationship that pushed you to invest all your energy in your next company or book? Or did the fact that you committed every ounce of psychic juice to your endeavor destroy your relationship with the "outside world" in the first place? It doesn't really matter.

Either way, the cycle may yield great art or great business, but a great life?

Doubtful.

I've dealt with this very tension many times in my own creative life. Each pursuit begs to become all-consuming. It teases you, then wraps its arm around you and lures you in. It's an amazing place to be, living on the marrow of conception and evolution. The world outside, a ghost of normalcy, can be easily forgotten.

That place where you live and breathe conception and evolution, it's been claimed, must exist. It's where great work comes from, where businesses are birthed, legends are made, and art comes to life. To visit this place and then return is necessary. But to believe that this place is a sustainable path to creation or to life is delusional. Trying to stay on that path for a sustained period of time always ends in disaster.

Not just because your relationships implode. They do. Not just because your body, your health, and your ability to check back into reality abandon you. They do. Not just because the demise of your outer world brings sadness, which is sand in the gears of productivity. It does.

Most of all, it's because you cannot sustain the level of conception and execution required to mount a breathtaking, lifetime-worthy body of work when all you do is work.

With rare exceptions, great creations—from paintings to companies to products to movies, songs, and books—don't come from life in a vacuum. One of the reasons McKee says great storytellers often don't hit their stride until later in life is because they have to have spent a massive number of hours mastering the craft; they also need to have lived enough outside the pursuit of their craft to have something worth saying—either that or they must have devoted themselves to going deep inside to cultivate what McKee calls a "ruthless self-knowledge" that they can draw upon.

It's the same with any endeavor, any quest to create something brilliant from nothing. It takes years to master a craft, from building a business to writing music. But craft alone doesn't get you there.

Genius requires craft plus insight.

Insight rarely comes while you are constrained to the work and only the work. Indeed, it most often comes when you step away from your work, when you spend time with others in seemingly unrelated worlds. When you sit, walk, and breathe into stillness. When you meditate. Talk. Listen. Love. Live. Be.

Counterintuitive as it sounds, it's the undoing that plants the seeds of the greatest doing. What I create in any one medium is made far richer by the fact that I spend considerable time outside that medium. It may mean my path to mastery takes longer. So be it. In the end, I create better businesses because I write. I write better books, essays, and posts because I relish my time as a dad, son, brother, husband, friend, yogi, student, and teacher.

I know this to be true. I've experienced it over and over, and I am mad about the people in my life. But still, when I drop into that single-minded creative place, I scare even myself. It's so easy to get lost in the place, despite the fact that, once pulled out, I'm keenly aware how much wonder grows out of my time engaged in other activities and relationships. Those seemingly unrelated experiences are as much a part of my creative life and creation processes as work more commonly labeled with those terms.

How exactly do you come back from that place? How do you find your way home when you've bound yourself to the mast and are heading into the bluffs? For the person driven by quest, is balance really possible?

It depends on how you define balance.

I don't believe in the myth of that magical place where everything exists in a state of persistent equilibrium. Life is messy. It's supposed to be. And that's a good thing. Hell, it's a wonderful thing, because the fray is where the greatest relationships and experiences are birthed.

But these same relationships and experiences bring with them the potential to pull our attention and sanity pendulums way out to one extreme and to allocate our energies in a way that is disproportionate to what we claim to hold dear in life.

Who has time to work out when you're on deadline?

We've got only so much runway before the company flames out.

You don't break into galleries or the iTunes top 10 or hit the *New York Times* best-seller list working half days.

I'll circle back to my loved ones later.

Showering? Heard of it.

Sometimes this disproportionate allocation of attention has to happen. When I'm launching a new company or online venture or finishing a book, I've always believed I needed to be in that bizarre altered reality, completely and utterly fixated on the quest. I have yet to meet the serious endeavor that didn't demand more as the "launch date" approached. But as I noted in the earlier conversation about bursts and ritual, meticulous attention to the way we create can make even this final push both more humane and less susceptible to obsessive withdrawal from reality.

IDENTIFY AND WORK WITHIN YOUR OPTIMAL CREATIVE STATES

Creative business consultant and co-founder of LateralAction.com Mark McGuinness offers another insight on the delicate balance between the compulsion of passion-driven work and the need to build an equally rich life outside your chosen medium.

We all have times during the day, says McGuinness, when we do our best work, and other times when we're relatively useless from both an insight and productivity standpoint. While these cycles can be altered with attention over time, without interference they are more or less baked into who we are, part of the same circadian rhythms that control alertness and sleep.

Even within those bigger rhythms, as Tony Schwartz noted, we also have an organic cap on our ability to focus. Ninety minutes is the outside window. And, honestly, that's being quite generous. Business strategist and *Be Unreasonable* (2007) author Paul Lemberg shared with me that his extensive work with hundreds of C-level executives and thousands of employees yielded a number closer to twenty-five to forty-five minutes. In a study he conducted of 500 small-business CEOs, Lemberg asked, "In a typical day, how much time do you spend working on things that make money or add real value to your business?"

The answer—a shocking two and a half hours a day.

My experience bears this out, though it also seems to be expandable through attention-building practices like AT. Either way, edge past your productivity window without taking some kind of substantial break to refuel your physical and psychological tanks and you're more or less serving time. You feel like you're being a good, committed, driven creator, but in reality you're just torturing yourself and those around you—and not getting a whole lot done.

How does this tie in to creative addiction and balance?

What might happen if you were to change your work windows to accommodate your most productive and creative rhythms, split those rhythms into bursts of intense focus lasting forty-five to ninety minutes, and work with breaks to rejuvenate between each? Then what if, when you know you're really not capable of doing your best work, instead of wallowing in *served time* because "that's what it takes to be great," you were to turn your attention to taking care of your body, your mind, your health, your relationships—your experience of life outside your primary creation medium.

Start by spending a few weeks really listening to and watching your rhythms to get a good sense for the parts of the day in which you're able to (1) do great work (2) with the greatest ease. Try working at different times of the day, maybe even rising early or staying up later to test a variety of windows.

If you've never done this, it's a pretty fascinating experiment. We all have these cycles, but if you work a standard day, you've most likely never paid attention to them. You may discover that your best work happens between 5 A.M. and 9 A.M.; maybe it's midday (which is far less common, even though it's when most of us are tasked with getting the most done), or it could even be early evening. When I was in law school, I did most of my studying and writing between 11 P.M. and 3 A.M., then slept through *Magnum, P.I.* every day at 3 P.M.

Once you've found your optimal creative window or windows (you may have a few), create a schedule that splits them into bursts of intense focus and attention. You may want to experiment, again, with ranges between forty-five and ninety minutes. For the better part of my life, I've been able to handle ninety minutes fairly readily. I recently developed tinnitus, and because of the sound that now lingers in my head all day and the impact it can have on my sleep, I've had to tune my window in to about thirty- to sixty-minute bursts and be vigilant about the need to adapt that on a daily basis. That's not a good thing or a bad thing; it's just a thing. What's important is that I was sensitive to it and, because of that, able to adjust my process so that I could continue to create effectively.

Rebuilding your work windows around your bigger creation rhythms and shorter focus cycles can make you immensely more productive. The impact extends far beyond your ability to do better work faster.

Productive creation rituals let you check back into your nonwork life. They give you both the time and the mind space to drop into that life far more often, spend more time there, take better care of yourself, and remind yourself how wonderful that place and its inhabitants are. Those experiences, in turn, make you into a better creator. Rather than creating a cycle of behavior that spirals you into obsession, you create a pattern that elevates the quality of your work, your very ability to work, and the richness of your life outside of work.

ESTABLISH CIRCUIT BREAKERS

Beyond retooling around natural rhythms, there's another very power-ful thing you can do. Set up circuit breakers to alert you to the need to come back.

Never go into that creative-obsessive cave without a rope, a timer, and someone at home who's been told to alert the authorities if you're not back at the agreed-upon time. You need to assemble both your venture team (if you have one) and your extra-venture team (aka your family and friends) and create a realistic understanding of the needs of that place *before you go there.*

- Define the triggers that signal you've been "under" for too long.
- Create feedback mechanisms that will tell you if and when you've been there too long.
- Define a vehicle that allows you to pull yourself out or alerts others to come looking.
- Get mutual agreement on these expectations, triggers, and mechanisms from those within the endeavor and those who sur-round it.

Doing this serves as a psychic circuit breaker. It lets you stop your attention and energy pendulum from swinging too far in one direc-tion and staying there too long. It helps you step outside yourself to see when that's really happening, then arms you with two abilities: (1) to send your pendulum swinging back through center, or (2) to ac-knowledge that your initial assumptions about the demands of this endeavor were off, so that you can establish new metrics, trigger points, and mechanisms and get renewed "sign-off" on them.

This is where the equanimity that Randy Komisar spoke of earlier plays a crucial role. It affords you the ability to step outside yourself, know when it's time to ask someone to throw you a line, and climb back out of a creative quest that's at risk of turning into a destructive abyss.

I do this with my wife in a fairly casual, yet critical way. I've built my work schedule around my ability to be very present with my family. That includes having one or two lunch dates with my wife every week. Even though, with a home office, we're around each other quite often, these lunches create more deliberate pauses in the day to have bigger-picture conversations about where we're going in life. They also create a mechanism to ask for and receive feedback on how my attention to what I'm building professionally is impacting not only my health and happiness, but also my wife's and daughter's health and happiness. These moments serve not only as regular feedback opportunities but also as circuit breakers that trigger a change in my attention, energy, and behavior when needed. They're invitations to consistently align my actions with my broader life values.

PUTTING IT TOGETHER

It's easy, as a creator, to fall into the habit of showing up and simply doing the work every day without ever stopping to examine whether your current direction is truly serving your muse, your greater life, and your community. An important part of the creative process of any individual or team is the ability to step out of the process on a regular basis and ask the big questions, to see the forest beyond the trees, and to make the big decisions based upon that larger exploration.

This chapter's focus has been on three of these big questions:

Are You Being Called to Create?

Understanding what's driving your compulsion to create not only your current endeavor but a body of work or a career is incredibly helpful as you make the bigger decisions and decide how much you are willing to sacrifice in the name of your quest. When you're called to create, you also live in your world differently and people respond to this, often rallying to support your endeavor in ways they would have been both unforeseeable and incomprehensible before you began.

When Should You Bail, Adapt, or Lean In?

This is one of the toughest questions every creator faces. It begins with an understanding of whether what you're working on feels like a calling—the thing you can't not do—or a project. If it's the former, you may find yourself committing to it, regardless of its ability to lead to mastery or in some way generate enough income to allow you to live well in the world. You do it because, at that moment in time, you believe that's what you can't not do. And if you're looking for it to translate to income but the conventional approach isn't working out, you either explore less-conventional paths to money or make a conscious decision that the intrinsic rewards of the quest offset the sacrifice.

If your current endeavor is more akin to an "interesting project" or a desire to serve a market or need, and you don't feel a strong connection to the specific medium, model, or product, you're more likely to find comfort, as you move deeper into the endeavor, in relying on the data that can replace leaps of faith as a guide for your decisions about viability and the need to adapt or pivot to stay alive.

Has Your Quest Become a Life-Gutting Addiction?

Creating something from nothing can become an all-immersive endeavor, consuming nearly every waking hour of your life and, without intervention, estranging you from life outside the quest. Be sure to set up a system of checks, balances, and vehicles that are designed to alert you when you're staying under too long and that then allow you to pull yourself back out into the world.

9

OWN THE STORY LINE

IT'S GO TIME for Deb Ng. More than 3,000 people pour into the massive Mandalay Bay Resort and Hotel in Las Vegas to experience three days handcrafted by her and her team. Ng is the Conference Director for BlogWorld and New Media Expo, the largest social media gathering in the world. Along with founders Rick Calvert and Dave Cynkin, she's spent the better part of the past year selecting the faculty of 300 or so presenters and overseeing the logistics of this mammoth event.

Her job, on paper, is simple: create an experience that delights everyone. Because she's also an active blogger and social media evangelist, Ng's name is very publicly attached to the event. If people love it, she'll know. And if they hate it, she'll know—to the potential tune of thousands of people blogging, tweeting, and updating their Facebook pages to report as much. There is no hiding in the clear waters of social media.

The pressure to deliver sounds insane, the possibility of public ridicule crushing. Who on Earth would take this on? Clearly it must be someone with a will of steel and the toughest skin on the planet. One of those natural fear alchemists.

But it's not. Deb Ng, in fact, is very human. She is very affected by others' opinions, happiness, and potential wrath. She holds herself to incredibly high standards for the work she does. It's part of what makes her so good at it. In a conference the size of the BlogWorld expo, things go wrong, big and small, all the time. But Ng just rolls with it. She feels the uncertainty, the exposure to judgment, the potential for loss, and the anxiety that rides along with it just as anyone else would who runs an event of that size. But those potential negatives are tempered and largely transformed into fuel by her ability to reframe the context and story lines around them.

Adding positive context, Ng loves what she does and who she does it with. Ng told me she's never felt as "in her element" as she does when she's working with her team to co-create an event around a topic she loves to evangelize for. Sure, things will go wrong, people will yell and scream, technology will fail, people will drop the ball. Rather than allow these things to derail her, she reframes these challenges as experiences and information that will help make next year's event even better. In her mind, this isn't so much a one-shot deal as it is a journey that will build and unfold for years. It's all about learning and serving. That "reframe" doesn't eliminate the emotions but rather gives it a different context, a different story line that allows her to lean into it and move through the uncertainty, exposure, and risk with more ease. That shift alone is pretty powerful.

There is also another story line running in Ng's head. It's about the world she left behind to do what she's doing now. In her former life, Ng worked for a large corporation in the publishing industry. It helped pay the bills, but it emptied her out. That's a world she never wants to be forced to return to. The more successful she becomes in her own creative endeavors, the more she learns and the better she does in her position as conference director, the more confident she becomes in the longevity of her current path and the notion that she's here to stay.

These alternative story lines provide fuel to inspire the work she needs to succeed in her current role. Beyond that they reframe the potentially anxiety-provoking side of her work in a way that largely disempowers the giant, lingering questions that punctuate every day until the last person has cleared out of the conference and she's on the plane home . . . already thinking of ways to improve next year's experience.

In a 2010 article in the online magazine fear.less, Rosamund Zander wrote beautifully about the way she reframed not only fear of judgment, but full-fledged actual judgment as something positive that fuels rather than paralyzes her:

> I remember when writing *The Art of Possibility*, the Harvard Business School sent out an early draft to readers before I felt it was ready to go. The comments we received back from the readers were pretty negative, and it surprised me that I was very interested in those negative comments and in what others had to say. I didn't quite understand it at the time, but I thought, "If they haven't understood what I'm trying to say, then perhaps I haven't conveyed it as well as I could have." So I saw it as their comments actually gave me clues on how to communicate my ideas better. With that perspective, even the most negative reader appeared to me to be on my team. I was surprised at how little the "criticism" hurt, that it didn't go too deep, and realized that I wasn't knocked over by it, but that it was useful for me.

Doing this gave the criticism a different context—a different story line. That's primarily what reframing is all about: looking at the facts, taking yourself out of the middle, and asking how you can view them in a different light, one that empowers rather than shuts you down. How can you change the context, the story, and the "frame" you've automatically wrapped around it? Where is the gift in the circumstance that's possessing you?

Reframing may seem a bit like pop-psychology "keep your chin up" voodoo, but it's really just an overlay of a concept that crosses a wide range of philosophical teachings as well as modern-day therapeutic modalities.

Reframing, in the world of psychology, is better known as an example of cognitive reappraisal, changing the story or message around fear-inducing stimuli to alter your emotional response. In a study published in 2002 in the *Journal of Cognitive Neuroscience*, a team led by Kevin Ochsner used functional magnetic resonance imaging to measure changes in the brain during reappraisal. Ochsner found that cognitive reappraisal activates the prefrontal cortex, the part of the brain implicated in self-regulation, and decreases activation of the brain's amygdala, the seat of fear and anxiety. Reframing literally changes the way your brain processes the experience, tamping down the fear and anxiety that might come as an automatic response to uncertainty, risk, and exposure to judgment.

This study helps explain why well-formed creative hives can change the fear dynamic and foster strength in the face of high stakes and great uncertainty. It allows participants to tell a different, "we're all in this together, and criticism is good" story. And it showcases a subcategory of reappraisal known as normalizing—framing an experience around the understanding that what you're going through is normal for people in such a situation. This awakening is yet another way to tell a story that reduces the experience of fear and anxiety without actually altering the circumstance.

Reframing is also a teaching that crosses nearly every philosophical lineage for thousands of years, especially those that have grown out of Eastern traditions. A wonderful Buddhist parable illustrates the power of a good reframing.

In a small village, the story goes, lived an old farmer. He awoke one morning to discover that his horse had run away. The news circulated through the town, and his neighbor paid a visit and offered condolences, saying, "What a shame."

"Maybe yes, maybe no," said the farmer.

The next day, the horse returned, bringing with it five wild horses.

"What a blessing," said the neighbor.

"Maybe yes, maybe no," said the farmer.

The following morning, the farmer's young son tried to ride one of the wild horses, was thrown, and broke his leg. "What a shame," said the neighbor.

"Maybe yes, maybe no," said the farmer.

That evening, high-ranking officials from the army arrived, enlisting every able-bodied young man and taking them off to war. The farmer's son, however, was left behind.

"What a blessing," said the neighbor.

"Maybe yes, maybe no," said the farmer.

Reframing takes quite a bit of practice. It's not easy to cultivate the ability to step outside of yourself and see beyond what often appears to be the only possible interpretation of any given circumstance, especially when you're mired in emotion, fear, and anxiety. The ability to cultivate a state of relative equanimity, often through some form of AT, lays a strong foundation for reframing (notice how many roads keep pointing back to AT as an essential practice for the creative life). For many, a qualified guide or therapist, at least early on, can make the process more accessible.

As a starting point, ask what other story lines you can create around your current endeavor that allow you to reframe it in a way that mobilizes, rather than paralyzes you.

A SPECIAL REFRAME: GOING TO ZERO

One of the greatest fears of creators is the fear of failure. But that term is pretty fuzzy. It's more of a catchall phrase that includes (1) fear of judgment (what happens when you crash and burn), (2) intolerance for uncertainty, and (3) fear of what most people would consider extreme loss. We'll use "going to zero" as a shorthand phrase to describe that trilogy.

What we're really talking about here is the anxiety that sets in when you envision yourself losing a solid enough chunk of money, time, energy, prestige, respect, or reputation that the fall would, in your mind, spell disaster.

An artist might experience this as the fear that a show doesn't sell a single piece of work, generates terrible reviews, and is so reviled by his peers and by collectors that the artist ends up shunned from the art world and exiled to selling pens on the subway for life. An entrepreneur might envision a scenario in which she leverages everything she owns and stakes the family's savings on her success; then the business explodes, she loses all her money and has to sell the house, and her partner, friends, colleagues, and peers abandon her. For an accomplished professional, CEO, or executive with a great track record and successful business, "going to zero" might be a failed project that ends up costing the company a huge amount of money, prestige, power, and competitive advantage and likely the job of the person leading the endeavor.

The extreme loss element of going to zero, though, is the easiest fear to quantify; it's the monster you can name. And once you can name it, you can tame it and reframe it along with the other fears that ride along with it. So let's explore how that reframe works.

When we think about going to zero, instead of just creating a realistic scenario, saying, "Okay, this is what happens and I'll get through it," we create a doomsday scenario. We start spinning in our heads:

"Oh, my God, if this thing collapses, I'm going to lose everything—my home, my relationships. I'm probably going to get thrown out of the country club. Everyone I've ever known since kindergarten will hate me. They're going to take away all my possessions. I'll have to eat five-for-a-buck noodles and live on the street for the rest of my life. Everything I've worked to build will evaporate in a moment."

Failing at any quest, especially when it's done in plain view, hurts. But the typical doomsday scenario most people create takes what is often a very small likelihood of recoverable pain and ramps it through the roof, bringing crushing levels of fear and anxiety along with it.

Then we do something even more destructive. We take that doomsday scenario and hit spin. In the typical way our brains work, repetition breeds belief. This phenomenon has been demonstrated many times over in experiments with both children and adults. We can start with a thought, a fact, a scenario, or a vision, and in our minds, regardless of whether it's based in truth, the more we repeat it, the more we believe it to be the absolute truth, the only possible outcome. Not *a* model of the world, but *the* model of the world. The more we buy into the assumption that this is the only possible outcome, the more we are overcome with fear and anxiety.

The net effect is paralysis. You can't move. If you haven't yet begun, it stops you from starting. If you're in the middle of creating something, it retards all forward movement. And if you've already experienced a certain level of success, it stops you from continuing to take risks and innovating on the level that got you where you are.

That alone is immensely destructive to your ability to create great work. But there's another bit of fallout that's even more insidious. When you enter the doomsday spin zone, you get so caught up in your own mental crud you lose the ability to ask the questions that would let you reframe going to zero, to reappraise the scenario and create a story line that mobilizes rather than paralyzes.

Before you go spinning into your next crash-and-burn fest, take a step back and walk through the going-to-zero scenario in a more em-powering way by asking and answering three critical questions that allow you to reframe the going-to-zero scenario in a different light.

Question 1: What If I Go to Zero?

Here's where you get to name your monster. It's important to ask this question. What if I go to zero, or even just end up losing something that will hurt an awful lot?

Instead of creating a fantastical doomsday scenario, create a very realistic scenario. Write it out. Create a picture. Make it a movie. Make it as vivid as you can. But that's only half of the exercise. The other half is to add another question: "How will I recover?" Give equal attention to that picture. Plot out exactly what you will do to bring yourself back.

I've been blessed with my share of professional crashes. Money, time, energy, passion—poof. Gone. It hurt like hell. But what I discovered, what most people and certainly most creators discover, is that it's not the end of the world. When you think about the risk of going to zero or losing a serious chunk of whatever it is you fear losing, name it, quantify it, but also quantify your road back. Doing that alone goes a long way toward disempowering the fear of going to zero. Because you realize almost everything is recoverable.

Many of the world's greatest creators, from traditional artists to entrepreneurs and global business builders, have gone to zero or func-tional zero—the loss of a big enough chunk of money, reputation, power, opportunity, or material goods to create the experience of ex-traordinary loss—and come back, sometimes more than once. In the bizarre universe of tech start-ups, I've even heard of venture capital-ists who won't fund a founder who's never endured and been steeled by the process of flaming out.

None report being at the bottom as fun. Indeed, in my last company, I dropped a lot of time, money, and energy into launching a franchise division and trying to make it work before realizing the fundamental model wasn't working the way I wanted it to, nor was it something that, once field-tested, I felt good about scaling. So I folded the division and lost a lot of money and time. It took me a few years to dig my way out of that hole. But I did, and the experience had an unexpected benefit. It gave me the confidence to realize that I had within me the ability to reach for big visions and, if I failed, to recover.

For many entrepreneurs, artists, and organizational innovators, the experience of going to zero releases within them the freedom to rebuild in a way they'd never have given themselves the latitude to explore had they never been stripped of their prior success.

In her 2008 Harvard commencement speech, Harry Potter author J. K. Rowling spoke to this experience with extraordinary clarity about what she experienced after she'd hit rock bottom both personally and financially:

> I was set free, because my greatest fear had been realized, and I was still alive, and I still had a daughter whom I adored, and I had an old typewriter and a big idea. And so rock bottom became the solid foundation on which I rebuilt my life. . . . The knowledge that you have emerged wiser and stronger from setbacks means that you are, ever after, secure in your ability to survive. You will never truly know yourself, or the strength of your relationships, until both have been tested by adversity. Such knowledge is a true gift, for all that it is painfully won, and it has been worth more than any qualification I ever earned.

Going to zero also has an intimate relationship with fear of judgment and the ability to create genius. We saw how fear of judgment decreases your tolerance for uncertainty and literally stunts your creative abilities. When you go to zero, all that falls away. When you arrive at the bottom, fear of judgment has nothing to grasp on to, because fear is an anticipatory emotion . . . and you're already there. You've cratered, you've been judged the whole way down. You no longer have to anticipate how it feels; you're living that state. How much worse could it really get if you tried to innovate your way out of the abyss and failed again? Why not try?

That, very often, is the place where extraordinary things happen. Without fear of judgment, your tolerance for uncertainty skyrockets, giving you the latitude to come up with or to try ideas you never had the will to try when you were on top of the world for fear of losing what you'd worked so hard to accomplish.

While going to zero is a horrible experience in so many ways, if you have the competence to have created enough and risen to a place glorious enough to make the fall painful, you'll still be able to leverage that same competence to pull yourself out, only that competence will be freed from the effect of the fear blinders that kept your highest level of creativity under lock and key until now.

Nobody wants to go to that place. But, with rare exceptions, it's possible to recover from there to create and rebuild on an entirely new level.

Going to zero also does one other thing: it largely disempowers, from that point forward, the stranglehold that the fear of failure had cast on you earlier. The pain that comes from fear of failure is based on the assumption not only that it hurts to hit bottom, but that your doomsday scenario is unrecoverable. The latter assumption—the belief that you'll live out your days destitute and cast out—is the source of the greatest pain.

When you've actually been to that place and battled your way back, your experience serves as proof that failure is, in fact, recoverable, and that your assumptions were wrong. This makes it far harder to reanimate your fear, knowing it's based on something you've experienced to be patently false.

Entrepreneurs and artists who've risen, crashed, then risen again often share a similarly disempowered outlook on fear of failure. Yes, it hurts, they'll say, but as J. K. Rowling observed, "The knowledge that you have emerged wiser and stronger from setbacks means that you are, ever after, secure in your ability to survive."

Question 2: What If I Do Nothing?

For a lot of people "What if I do nothing" seems like a throwaway question. But a truthful answer details a scenario that is downright horrifying, far more so than failure and recovery. In reality, there is no sideways in life—not in relationships, not in business, not in spiritual growth, not in the quest to build something brilliant from nothing. There's only up or down. The notion that you can just coast through life in neutral is a fallacy constructed to rationalize inaction.

If you are a bit overweight, overtired, overstressed, estranged from friends, lovers, family members, or colleagues now and you do nothing to change the scenario, five, ten, or fifteen years from now you will not be equally dissatisfied with these parts of your life. Without nourishment or action, your health, your relationships, your interests, passions, professions, and appetite for quest will slowly decline to the point of utter annihilation. If you fancy yourself a painter and you dream of creating massive postmodern canvases that hang in the great rooms of important collectors, but instead disdainfully earn your rent white-labeling illustrations on place settings, do you really think that twenty years from now you'll remain merely disdainful? No. You're far more likely to slide, year after year, into frustration, futility, and despair. Because there is no neutral.

We see this phenomenon as well in entrepreneurs, artists, and corporate leaders who've achieved substantial success, then pulled back into neutral out of fear of losing the power, prestige, reputation, money, and freedom they've amassed by taking the big risk, leaning into uncertainty, and exposing themselves to judgment. Instead of constantly moving the ball forward, they turn most of their energies toward not losing whatever ground they've been able to claim. They replace innovation with complacency and inevitably suffer the consequences of the sideways slide.

I've watched this unfold repeatedly in the health, fitness, and lifestyle industry, a world I know well, having launched, built, and sold two companies in that space. And I've blogged about it extensively. The business model for mainstream health clubs is built on automated monthly payments. The supposed beauty of this model is that it shifts the burden of reselling and reearning the membership fee away from the club and instead places the burden of termination on the member. The billing stops only when the member proactively says, "No more." This model allows health clubs to do something very few other businesses can do: start and stay cash-flow-positive and have a strong sense of future cash flow. But all too often that same sense of cash-flow security engenders institutionalized complacency, disincentivizes innovation, remarkability, and delight. It leaves staff uninspired and leads to an elevated annual dropout rate. It also requires you to spend vastly more money on marketing to drive a constant stream of new people into a business model that's changed very little in thirty years. It makes you susceptible to being picked off by upstarts who aren't wedded to the way you operate and aren't paralyzed by a fear of losing what they've already built.

This very thing is happening in the fitness world right now. Progressive, experimental, highly adaptive new approaches to serving fitness, lifestyle, and community needs are making rapid inroads and leaving the big stalwarts in the dust. Great examples include CrossFit, with its strong focus on community, high-level engagement, and participation, and a wide range of functional movement. Another is SoulCycle, a company that's redefining indoor cycling with small-footprint, high-touch, experience-driven studios. These places charge top-of-the-market fees and are attracting people who wouldn't pay even a fraction of that amount to exercise at one of the stagnating big-box facilities.

By no means is the "sideways is good enough" mentality limited to the fitness industry. In fact, the challenging economy is fueling a mass movement to this position. Concerned about job security, employees who built careers on the back of innovation across a wide spectrum of industries are increasingly unwilling to take bold, creative action. Nobody wants to guess wrong in a climate where money is short and jobs are shorter. The net effect—a stifling of the very risk taking, innovation, and action in the face of uncertainty that fueled earlier success—spells troubling times ahead for many companies that don't reaffirm their commitment to a culture of innovation, and not just in words, but in actions.

In art, business, and entrepreneurship, there is no coasting. There is no neutral. No sideways. It's a myth, an illusion. There's only up or down. Leading or trailing.

Which means that if you're teetering on the edge of happiness, health, liquidity, and contentment now and if you're stuck in a "do nothing to change" scenario, then ten, twenty, or thirty years from now, your creative life, your business, and your body of work will likely be somewhere between really unpleasant and really dead.

Let's expand this idea out into your role as the creator of your life. If you leave key parts of your life unaddressed over time, here's what's likely to happen:

- Nagging pain becomes chronic, acute, and debilitating.
- Unrewarding work becomes soulless, life-sucking agony.
- Passable health becomes obesity, disease, and, for many, early death.

- Relationships that are unattended to become estranged, angry, bitter, dysfunctional, and nonexistent.
- Your currently "passable" life becomes increasingly painful as you enter the long, slow slide toward death.

Create a vivid, realistic picture of how a neutral scenario will look in your work and life five, ten, or twenty years from now. Without fail, that's a story line to run from.

Question 3: What If I Succeed?

It's time to complete the going-to-zero reframe with a final question, one that allows you to create a story line of success. This is where we have fun. So far, we've been talking about reframing and disempowering the crash, and about owning up to the true pain of complacency. But now we talk about hope. Now we move to the other side of the equation.

We ask the final question. What if I succeed?

If you have a very precise vision for what you'd like to create from the beginning, here is where you lay it out. See it, feel it, touch it, smell it, taste it. Make it as sensory and alive as possible. Picture yourself in that place. What are you working on? With whom? Where are you? What does your day look like? For some it's possible to get very specific. For others, especially in the earliest stages of an endeavor, it's more about bigger-picture qualities. If you feel compelled to create great art, you may not have a clear picture of the vehicle or medium quite yet, but you can imagine how it will feel to create and present art that moves people to tears. If you're an entrepreneur, you may not know what you're going to create or how you're going to solve the problems of the marketplace, but you can envision what it will feel and look like to have created a solution that blows peoples' minds and changes their lives, to have created an organization steeped in mentoring and compassion and a culture of joy, innovation, and energy. You can imagine where your workplace will be and what it will look like once you've accomplished what you dream of doing.

Paint that picture. Make it real. And make that your predominant story line.

Stilling and Spinning

Now revisit all three scenarios: your going-to-zero scenario, your do nothing scenario, and your success scenario.

Acknowledge the potential for pain created by the first scenario, but also the power of your recovery scenario and the potential for even greater creative space and success. Set that story line aside.

Now take the sideways story line, drink it in, feel it viscerally, and understand its genuine impact on your life should that become the story line of your creative life. Then set it aside too. But revisit it once a month as reinforcement.

Finally, take your success story line. Add more detail. What does it feel like, sound like, taste like? What do you see? Write it out. Take pictures. Strip it down to the smallest actions you can take today that inspire joy. Then take that story line and hit spin.

Reframe complete. Buh-bye, monster.

PUTTING IT TOGETHER

While there is no way to avoid uncertainty, risk, and exposure in the quest to make great things, with practice we can change the stories we tell around the experiences that scare us in a way that empowers action and dampens the experience of fear and anxiety. Start by asking what other stories you can tell about what's going on. What other potential models might explain a given scenario? How can you reappraise the situation to experience it as mobilizing rather than paralyzing?

In the case of what I've identified as going to zero, be sure to explore the three key questions as well:

- What if fail, then recover?
- What if I do nothing?
- What if I succeed?

For some, once they are armed with a basic framework and enough proof that the approach works, reframing becomes a relatively intuitive process. For others, the challenge is too much to explore alone. If that is you, I encourage you to reach out to a qualified professional to help guide you through this process. If you are having trouble adopting many of the techniques and strategies shared in this book, it's a good idea to reach out to a qualified professional to help assess your current state of mind and to guide the development of your personal approach and practice.

If you have even the slightest question about whether the emotions you are experiencing are a normal part of a substantial creative effort or something bigger and potentially psychologically destructive, err on the side of getting the help you may need. Find and defer to the guidance of a qualified mental-health-care professional. No book is an adequate substitute for professional therapeutic guidance.

10

BRING IT HOME

WE ARE WIRED from birth to want answers and hard data. Uncertainty is okay, as long as it exists in someone else's life or we don't have to do anything about it. But as soon as we're challenged to own it and then act in the face of it, with rare exceptions we run from it. Because running *at* it terrifies us. We're scared of the discomfort that comes with opening doors without knowing what's behind them. Scared of being judged if it's a monster. Scared of having to pick up the pieces and rebuild if we go to zero. Even scared of hitting the jackpot. And beyond the fear, we just plain hate the persistent anxiety that rides along with continually leaning into the unknown. Without intervention, we experience it as anywhere from discomfort to outright suffering.

The problem is, if you strive to create anything—be it a book, a business, a blog, a collection, a body of work, or a career that is defined by brilliance—uncertainty, risk of loss, and exposure to judgment are necessary parts of the quest. They'll ebb and flow and move toward certainty as each project or new endeavor takes shape.

But even then, in larger context of the creative life, each end signals a new beginning. And with each new beginning, should you continue to choose the path of innovation, growth, and impact, comes a renewed wave of uncertainty, risk, and exposure. It never really entirely ends . . . until you end.

When you run from uncertainty, you end up running from life. From evolution. From growth. From wisdom. From friendship. From love. From the creation of art, services, solutions, and experiences that move beyond what's been done before to illuminate, serve, solve, and delight in a way that matters. In a way that makes you come alive and that people will feel and remember.

Sociologist Immanuel Wallerstein said in a talk he gave at a 1997 forum in Prague:

> Uncertainty is wondrous, and . . . certainty, were it to be real, would be moral death. If we were certain of the future, there could be no moral compulsion to do anything. We would be free to indulge every passion and pursue every egoism, since all actions fall within the certainty that has been ordained. If everything is uncertain, then the future is open to creativity, not merely human creativity but the creativity of all nature. It is open to possibility, and therefore to a better world.

Certainty, beyond the fact that you were born and you will one day die, does not exist. It's a fiction created to entice us to act. So we work to eliminate as much uncertainty as we can as quickly as possible. But when we eliminate uncertainty, we necessarily eliminate novelty. And novelty is the starting point for creation and innovation. In eliminating uncertainty, we kill our shot at brilliance. We become derivative. All in the name of not having to learn to live with butterflies.

I am not a natural-born fear alchemist. Increasingly, I doubt the existence of such a creature. I feel fear and uncertainty in my brain, my gut, and my entire body. I shake before I go onstage to speak. My stomach spins when I'm working on something I know will expose to the world the dorky, offbeat essence of who I am. Launching companies, books, and other ventures takes a ton of work, and for years, as I staged a launch I would pace, rant, swear, stare, plot, and devour bricks of Green & Black's 85% dark chocolate. Part of that feeling was brutal. But one of the greatest gifts in writing this book has been the impact that it's had on my own creation process and life. On the way I see and experience fear, uncertainty, anxiety, quest, and creation.

It's fueled me to return to the personal practices I'd all but abandoned over the last few years. That alone has been a gift, helping to rekindle a growing sense of equanimity and ability to reframe as signposts of progress, innovation, and creation what for years I'd experienced as suffering. I still feel fear, uncertainty, and anxiety, but I process it differently. I'm discovering how to not only survive it but to seek it out in the name of creating something extraordinary.

The greatest creators in any field take action. They move their endeavors forward, but at the same time they maintain an expansive view of where the endeavor is "calling" them to go. People may be enthusiastic over the *results*, but for many of these creators, the dynamism of the *process* itself is where the art really happens. The final product is a souvenir. They're ready to move on. I know it's that way for me.

When I finally got this, it changed the way I chose to create. It made me plan and work like crazy to get "input." But then instead of creating the most detailed plan of action as early as possible and executing on it doggedly, I decided to slow things down and create a living framework of core ideas and questions to be explored and answered.

I turned my own creative process into more of a dance than a race.

I built certainty anchors more deliberately into my life and my work. I created more systematic routines around basic lifestyle activities, then rebuilt work-oriented creation efforts around a series of intense bursts interspersed with activities that would give both my brain and my body a chance to recover and refuel.

I created and leaned on my own creation hive, an inner circle of like-minded writers, marketers, and entrepreneurs who I knew were insanely smart, compassionate, driven, and abundance oriented— meaning we each viewed the others' successes as our own and rallied to support them.

Leveraging technology, I created my own private creation tribe, which was in part a subset of my already rich online community but also included a number of new voices drawn to share in my process and journey. I shared ideas, insights, and experiences; led private conference calls and Q&As; and opened what is normally a very cloistered process in exchange for the occasional request for insights, ideas, and information. That was our bargain. And I experienced, firsthand, the need to balance the exchange with the need to maintain leadership over the process. I will likely bring this same group into the process as I explore creating and launching a variety of future artistic and entrepreneurial endeavors.

A number of colleagues have become mentors and confidants. I have no lack of professional heroes. And my wife still is the bedrock of my ability to do what I do. She is my champion.

Though I taught yoga and meditation for many years, upon selling my last company I'd largely walked away from them. Truth told, my practice of both had become sporadic long before that. Recommitting to a twice-a-day meditation practice has allowed me to find what Randy Komisar identified as a "keel" in the storm of life, as well as a place of stillness in which to cultivate ideas and insights and let them grow into actions and then endeavors. I've begun to reclaim my love of movement and exercise. And I've spent a considerable amount of time exploring the story lines I've created around my various adventures and practicing ways to reframe them in a way that inspires action and creative risk and invites feedback and innovation.

Most important, I've placed a keen focus on how my professional life interacts with my ability to create the truest legacy I know: that of a loving, present, and engaged father, husband, family member, and friend. Yes, I want to be known someday as a writer. Someone who built things that made a difference. Someone who illuminated and led. Someone who mattered. But before anything else, I want to always know, love, and serve those closest to me in a way that matters to them.

Doing all of these things pushed me—a lot. But they've also allowed me to lean with greater comfort than ever before into the uncertainty and fear that must be part of the quest to create something brilliant from nothing. I am no longer just an artist, an entrepreneur, or a creator. I'm training, and likely forever will be, in the alchemy of fear.

It's my greatest hope that this book provides both the inspiration and the foundation needed for you to do the same.

CHAPTER SUMMARIES

1. Why Uncertainty Matters

Every quest to create something bold starts with a question, a hunch, or an idea. There are far more unknowns than knowns, and that's the way it needs to be. The only way to know all the answers, all the brushstrokes, words, codes, models, forms, shapes, and data points in advance is to seek to create something that has already been created before. Which means you're no longer creating; you're replicating, turning out work that is derivative, and that's not what we're here for.

We are in this game to bring to life art, business, ideas, products, services, companies, and experiences that are signals, not noise—objects and endeavors that in some way add to the experience of business, culture, humanity, and life. That requires us to live with uncertainty and its trusted sidekicks: risk of loss and exposure to judgment. These qualities are signposts, at least in the early stages of any endeavor, that what you're doing is worth the effort. That it matters to you and, one hopes, to others.

For these reasons, we need to develop the ability to tolerate uncertainty and its companions, and to invite and at times even amplify them in the name of creating on a level that matters. The problem is, "living in the question" isn't so easy.

2. What Uncertainty Does to Us

Uncertainty causes pain. With rare exceptions we experience living in the question as suffering, anxiety, and fear. Sadly, that is our natural default state. It's hardwired into our brains. Experiencing movement toward the unknown as anxiety and fear may have served an important survival role in a different time. But these days it stops us from taking the actions needed to launch the endeavors, quests, projects, and ideas that fill our days with meaning, even to the point of driving us away from what we believe we're on the planet to do.

It's not just uncertainty we run from, it's also the fear of judgment and risk of loss that ride along with it. Bundled together, they create a basket of angst and anxiety that paralyzes some people, slows the process of others to a crawl, and stunts the creative abilities of those who nevertheless find the will to act.

All of this conspires to make us run to do whatever we can to eliminate the bad feelings. We rush to create certainty and eliminate risk and judgment, but as part of that process we unintentionally snuff out our ability to create genius.

What if there was another way?

3. The Myth of the Fearless Creator

Not everyone is shut down by uncertainty, risk of loss, and fear of judgment. All around us, we hear stories of writers, painters, dancers, coders, entrepreneurs, and innovative corporate teams who appear to have a near-superhuman ability to dance with the elements of creation that terrify most people. In doing so, they create stunning art, businesses, solutions, and experiences.

Are these people just freaks of nature? Are they somehow wired differently? What gives them the ability to lean into the emotions and experiences that shut most other people down?

It turns out that, with rare exceptions, it's much more about nurture than it is about nature. There is a series of situational changes, personal practices, and shifts in mind-set that radically alter the way many of these people experience the same open-ended circumstances that shut most others down. Some people build these things into their lives, with great deliberation, as scaffolding that allows them to lean more deeply into the journey. Others adopt them without even recognizing that's what they're doing.

What are these things that would allow us to become fear alchemists, to transform the circumstances that would normally terrify us into fuel for creative brilliance?

4. Find Your Certainty Anchors

Certainty anchors are experiences—ones that either happen naturally or that you build intentionally into your life—that serve as a source of psychological bedrock. They allow you to take more risks and embrace uncertainty in your work with more confidence in the name of creating better, deeper outcomes.

Rituals and routines are primary examples, both within the broader context of life and within the narrower process of your current endeavors. They also serve a secondary role. We all come to the process of creation with certain orientations and preferences. Some people are more drawn to white pages and big ideas. Others are more comfortable with refinement, process, and production. Intelligent certainty anchors, especially well-constructed, burst-driven rituals and routines, help counter the resistance that comes when you lean into the side of the creation process that tends to war with your creative orientation.

5. Build Your Hive

Along with developing a kinship with uncertainty, one of the greatest challenges in the life of a creator is handling judgment, criticism, and feedback. Most people try to avoid them because their prior experience of them has included discomfort. Criticism, however, is not only essential to moving your creative endeavor forward; in practical experience, it's impossible to avoid, especially if you're doing something that's never been done before or are taking action that makes people around you uncomfortable about their unwillingness to do the same.

Finding or creating a judgment-leveling creation hive can be an incredibly effective vehicle that can open you to the feedback you need to grow your abilities and your endeavor as efficiently as possible. A creative hive can be especially powerful when you experience it in conjunction with engaged mentors, champions, and heroes. But beware the hive that kills. When you put enough people in a contained space, the emotion, mood, or attitude of the leaders or influencers sets the tone for the entire group. Be very alert to this dynamic and work to find or create an environment that buoys all creative ships, rather than burn them to a crisp.

6. Socializing Creation

It is impossible to create anything substantial, novel, and capable of serious impact without embracing a fair amount of uncertainty and making a lot of leaps of faith in the early days. Traditionally, it would take months, years, or even decades for these leaps to fully prove or disprove themselves, leaving you with often major, painful course corrections to make along the way.

For those who dare to wade into the waters of technology, it is now possible to dramatically shorten the time needed to arrive at certainty and to reallocate the way you test your ideas, gather information, build on what works, and eliminate what does not. If you blend "lean methodology" or other feedback-driven technologies into your process, you can rapid-prototype, release, gather feedback, re-prototype, and re-release incredibly quickly and with smaller and smaller changes. This sequence alters not only the process of creation, but the deeper psychology, adding certainty more often and in smaller chunks and fueling action.

This approach can be adapted not just for tech start-ups and business, but for the traditional arts as well, as many writers and musicians are now demonstrating.

Socializing creation also raises a host of big questions. What happens when you elevate end users to the level of co-creators? Should their opinions really matter? Can you still be a tastemaker or paradigm-shifter? Who gets credit, and should there be an exchange of value?

7. Train Your Brain

Beyond changes in environment, culture, workflow and the broader framework of your day, there are certain daily personal practices that can be immensely useful in simultaneously building the stillness needed to lean into uncertainty and ramping up creativity, cognitive function, mood, and productivity.

Attentional training (AT)—training your brain in the art of focused awareness—has been practiced in various forms for thousands of years. Modern approaches include many forms of meditation, relaxation response training, and movement. Claims about powerful alterations in mental state and abilities have been bandied about for millennia, but over the past forty years, scientists have developed a substantial body of research validating many of these claims. Adopting such a practice can change not only your ability to create and experience the process with greater humanity, but also the very way you live in the world. Equanimity is an extraordinary tool for all aspects of life.

In addition to AT, there now exists a strong history of research supporting the importance of exercise not just as a vehicle for improved physical health, but as a key to an enhanced mind-set and better brain function. Research now shows that both exercise and AT are capable of growing brain cells, something thought impossible not too long ago. When they are practiced in harmony, exercise and AT are the strongest creation-force multipliers on the planet.

To these two practices, you will then adopt a growth mind-set and engage in process simulation. A growth mind-set values work over genetics as the heart of excellence and fundamentally alters the way you experience feedback, criticism, and judgment. Process simulation is an often-ignored approach to visualization that focuses on the process over the outcome, leading to a higher likelihood of daily action, especially in the early days of an endeavor, when it's nearly impossible to have a clear vision of the outcome.

8. See the Forest

Giant questions tend to loom in your mind throughout the life of a particular creative endeavor. How committed are you to the specific endeavor? Is it a project or a calling, the thing you can't not do? Understanding the difference informs the choices you make, but it also changes the way you act in a thousand tiny ways. It changes your personal energy and leads people either to buy in on an extraordinary level or to view your quest as something not all that important.

One of the bigger questions that often comes gallivanting back in every time a new major hurdle presents itself is whether to keep going, to change what you're doing, or to fold and shut down the endeavor altogether. Understanding whether you're being driven by a calling or by a current interest is critical in exploring intelligent answers to this question. Projects driven by a current interest or by business considerations often open up the need to rely more strongly on streams of data that replace your initial leaps of faith. On the other hand, a calling leads to another set of questions, driven by a "softer" though equally important exploration.

Any deeply meaningful endeavor also brings with it the opportunity to lose yourself in the quest, to go so far down the creation rabbit hole that, for all intents and purposes, your vision takes you into an addiction capable of destroying the other parts of your life. To counter this, it's important to establish a set of circuit breakers designed to allow you to come back from a quest that has turned into an abyss, to reconnect with the people and activities that add tremendous richness to life and serve as a source of fuel for even greater ideas when you return to the endeavor.

9. Own the Story Line

While we cannot completely extinguish the uncertainty and risk that come with creation (nor do we want to), another extraordinarily effective way to diminish that normal fear and anxiety is reframing—in therapeutic terms, cognitive reappraisal. This practice does nothing to change the circumstances that give rise to fear and anxiety; instead, it allows us to create and associate a different story line around those circumstances. Instead of defaulting to an automatic story that engenders negative emotion, we lean on the equanimity created through the practices described in chapter 7, Train Your Brain, to create a bit of psychic space, then ask what other interpretations might exist.

One of the most common destructive story lines creators tell is the going-to-zero story, in which they lose enough power, prestige, money, ability, and stuff to create deep, lasting pain. Many aspiring creators become paralyzed when thinking about their going-to-zero scenario. They focus only on the "unrecoverable doom" story line and in doing so never explore other questions, stories, and appraisals that would turn that scenario from a source of paralysis into a source of power and mobility.

10. Bring It Home

Uncertainty must be present in the quest to create anything deeply meaningful to you as the creator and, should you choose seek value from others in exchange for your creation, to the world. Over time, facts and actual experiences will replace leaps of faith and hunches, your endeavor will move closer to final form, and uncertainty will cede to certainty. Even then, the uncertainty about what you are building in the greater context of a career or body of work will likely remain.

While uncertainty must be present, especially in the early stages of a creative endeavor, our natural tendency is to run from and work to eliminate things that cause us pain. This leads us to short-circuit our ability to create genius in a number of ways. It may lead us to never start. It may make us push an endeavor forward too quickly because we can no longer handle not knowing how it's going to work out. Or it may lead us to overquestion every potential action, thus slowing the process to a near halt.

Whether you're an artist, entrepreneur, or innovation-driven team member, the ideas, strategies, and recommendations shared in the pages of this book will lay a foundation that will make the creation process both far more enjoyable and productive. They will arm you with the tools to create solutions, experiences, art, and outcomes on an entirely different level. And as an added benefit, many will also greatly enhance your experience of life beyond your endeavor.

ADDITIONAL RESOURCES

This book is filled with recommendations for productively embracing uncertainty. If you are comfortable tackling the suggestions alone, have at it. If you feel that you or your organization would benefit from a more structured approach to implementing many of the suggestions, here are some additional tools and resources to consider:

Creation Mind-set Audit

This free online tool—found at JonathanFields.com—walks you through a series of diagnostic questions that help you determine (1) where your biggest environmental, workflow, and individual creation mind-set gaps lie, and (2) where to focus your efforts to best optimize your environment and mind-set to fuel higher levels of creativity, productivity, innovation, and enjoyment. It is equally relevant for individual creators—like artists, writers, solo entrepreneurs—and teams and larger organizations.

Uncertainty: Fuel for Brilliance Workbook

This free downloadable PDF workbook—found at JonathanFields .com—tracks the chapters in this book, offering a set of guided questions and prompts to help you get the most out of the book, decide what changes to explore, and lay out a plan of action.

Online and On-Site Training

For a more hands-on or in-depth training experience tailored to you or to your organization's specific needs, you may also want to explore our live and virtual trainings and consulting. You can find more information on these at JonathanFields.com.

Speaking

To book Jonathan Fields for a speaking engagement, you can find more information at JonathanFields.com, or contact him via e-mail (booking@jonathanfields.com) or telephone (646-DRIVE-08).

CONVERSATION STARTERS

When I created the tagline for my blog—"Conversations at the crossroads of work, play, entrepreneurship & life"—I chose the first word with great deliberation. I want my blog to become a place where people come for great, illuminating conversation. To encourage this, I write many of my articles and posts as conversation starters, and it's not unusual for me to end up with tens of thousands of words of comments and conversation in response to a 1,000-word post. I love that. It's incredible to watch the discourse unfold, and I learn a tremendous amount from those conversations.

I wrote this book with the same intention—to provoke a new way of thinking about your creation process and a bigger conversation about the ideas you discover. Many of you may find those ideas contrary to some of your long-held assumptions. Others may find support and understanding for behaviors that have held them back, along with newfound tools and strategies to take action. Either way, use these ideas as a starting point not just for your own personal exploration, but for a conversation with anyone else involved in your creative endeavors.

Get together with a group of like-minded creators, or if you have the benefit of working in a group or team, bring them into the conversation. Read the book (chapter by chapter, if you like), then explore the following conversation starters and questions together. You will likely end up learning a great deal about one another, about yourself, and about how to improve both your individual and collective creation processes, make the journey far more enjoyable, and bring great things to life with more ease:

- How does uncertainty—not knowing how things will turn out, especially in the early days of an endeavor—make you feel?
- Does the nature of what you create allow you to easily quantify the odds and magnitude of success or failure? If not, how do you measure success? Failure?
- Do you do anything to help bolster your ability to embrace uncertainty and risk in the context of your creative process? If so, what? How has it been working?
- How do you generally handle being exposed to judgment, criticism, and feedback in the context of a creative endeavor? What could you potentially do differently that might allow you to benefit from regular feedback without feeling the pain of being judged?
- What is your creative modus operandi (CMO), the environmental preferences that put you in an optimal creative state? Compare your CMO with others to see what you have in common and how you differ.
  - ◊ Clothes
  - ◊ Sound
  - ◊ Light
  - ◊ Location
  - ◊ Directionality
  - ◊ Time of day

◊ Routine/spontaneous
◊ Long periods or short bursts
◊ Carry something to capture ideas on the fly?
◊ Squeaky clean or squalor
◊ Clean or dirty
◊ Solo or surrounded
◊ Digital or analogue
◊ What fuels you?
◊ Leaded or unleaded?
◊ Breaks
◊ Mind-set practices that fuel creation
◊ Movement practices that fuel creation

- Do you currently or have you ever worked in a hive-like creative environment? What were the benefits? What were the negatives? Describe the elements and energy of a creation hive that you believe would help inspire your best work. Compare your description with that of others.

- Have you built any certainty anchors, rituals, or routines into your life in general and/or into your creative process? If so, what are they? Were they intentional or did they just happen? Have you noticed how they affect your ability to create at the highest levels? How might you either adapt your current rituals and routines or create new ones to foster a greater ability to lean into uncertainty and push your process to the next level?

- Do you feel you have a clear creation orientation toward insight and ideation or toward refinement, expansion, and production? Are you more strongly drawn to or repelled by either of those two essential parts of the process? If you work on a team, is there a good balance of complementary orientations, or are most of the team members similarly orientated?

- Do you often find yourself having to work on the side of the creation process that tends to empty you out, without intervention? How have you handled this until now? How might you handle it more effectively moving forward?

- Is there some way to add elements of lean methodology to your endeavor or creative medium, even if it's not in any way related to technology? Can you create smaller but intelligible snippets of your bigger creations and solicit feedback before progressing with your larger endeavors? In your mind, do you have any business doing that, or does it bastardize and dilute both your process and the quality of what you create?

- How do you feel about elevating the people who might eventually experience or consume your creations to the level of providing valued input and potentially even co-creating? If you do bring these folks into the process, do they deserve shared credit and/or value? If so, who determines what that value is?

- Have you built any personal practices into your life that might allow you to create a stronger sense of grounding, equanimity, and calm in the face of uncertainty and risk? What are those practices? How often do you do them? Okay, now really, how often do you do them? What impact have they had? Based on your CMO and work schedule, what is the best time of day to do them? If you haven't explored any practices, can you commit to trying one (I would start with AT) during the time you have available?

- Do you approach work and life with more of a growth mind-set (success comes from work and feedback is critical) or a fixed mind-set (success comes from genes; feedback doesn't mean much because you've got what you've got)? How has your approach influenced your ability to create and to invite criticism into the process?

- Do you consider what you do a calling, or is it more of a current interest or job? How has this influenced your decisions about how much of your time, money, and energy you are willing to commit to bring the endeavor to life? How do you know when to hold, when to keep going but make changes, and when to fold?

- Do you ever find yourself so absorbed by an endeavor that you begin to lose touch with life outside the endeavor for extended periods of time? When that happens, do you ignore extra-endeavor relationships and activities that you love and value? Have you established circuit breakers to let you know that being down under for too long is having a destructive impact on the greater part of life you claim to hold dear? What are they? If you don't have circuit breakers, what can you put in place today?

- What are the stories you tell yourself about your current endeavor? What does it mean to you? What would it look like if you were to succeed? What would it look like if you failed? How would you recover if you did? If you are having trouble taking action, how else might you interpret your current circumstance or tell a different story around it that would mobilize you and fortify you against whatever fear and anxiety may be stopping you?

- How would it feel to know you were doing everything possible to do your best work and bring extraordinary creations to life? Do you feel you're doing that now? Are you willing to take the first step to begin today?

ACKNOWLEDGMENTS

There are, quite simply, no two people who have made this book more possible than my wife, Stephanie, and my daughter, Jesse. Their love, faith, willingness to embrace my ever-evolving journey, and their ability to keep me grounded and focused on what really matters is at the heart of my ability to create not only a meaningful living, but an extraordinary life. That gift is stunning.

My parents, sister, and friends have helped me find the confidence and freedom to be who I am and build what I build.

Wendy Sherman, my agent, has been a keel in the rapidly changing world of books. My editor, Courtney Young, and the entire team at Portfolio kept me intensely focused on value and craft, while giving me enough space to bring forth new ideas and processes.

To the many people who appear in this book as well as those who were kind enough to share their stories and ideas but were not able to be included—you all are my teachers, and I thank you for sharing your wisdom through your insights and the way you live your lives.

I thank fellow innovation instigators and members of my digital-water-cooler brain trust: Chris Guillebeau, Pam Slim, Charlie Gilkey, Sonia Simone, Tim Berry, Tony Schwartz, Gretchen Rubin, Erik Proulx, Debbie Stier, Stephen Johnson, Edward Boches, Danielle LaPorte, Lewis Howes, Leo Babauta, Lori Taylor, Sean Platt, Sarah Robinson, Derek Halpern, Bryan Franklin, Michael Ellsberg, Liz Strauss, Glen Stansberry, Michael Bungay Stanier, Susan Piver, Les McKeown, Ariane de Bonvoisin, Terry St. Marie, Chris Garrett, and dozens of others who inspire and challenge me to dig deeper, work harder, share more, love bigger, live more deliberately, and do great work.

Through some quirk of fate, I've also been blessed with an incredible gathering of people—from my private creation tribe, who helped guide and shape elements of this book, to the community on my blog, whose conversations consistently challenge and inform me, to my extended communities on Twitter and Facebook. Much gratitude to the tribes.

This train is only picking up steam from here.

INDEX

ABOUT THE AUTHOR

JONATHAN FIELDS is on a mission to humanize and empower the process of creation, helping individuals and organizations conceive and build better solutions, businesses, art, and lives in less time, with more joy and less effort. And he's doing it in a rather unusual way—from the inside out.

A former S.E.C./megafirm lawyer turned serial wellness-industry entrepreneur, author, and speaker, Fields has been featured in the *New York Times*, the *Wall Street Journal*, Bloomberg *BusinessWeek*, FastCompany.com, *Entrepreneur*, *USA Today*, *People*, CNBC, *Fox-Business*, Inc.com, *Yoga Journal*, *Vogue*, *Self*, *Fitness*, *Mind + Body*, *O Magazine*, and thousands of other media outlets, books, and Web sites. He writes an acclaimed *AdAge Power 150* blog on innovation, entrepreneurship, and lifestyles at JonathanFields.com, and his earlier book, *Career Renegade: How to Make a Great Living Doing What You Love* (2009) was named a Top 10 Small Biz Book by Small Business Trends and a Top 5 Summer Read by MSNBC's Your Money.

Over the last ten years, Fields has researched, developed, and shared a growing synthesis of strategies and practices designed to allow people and organizations to reframe and embrace uncertainty, risk of loss, and exposure to judgment not as sources of fear, anxiety, and paralysis, but as catalysts for innovation, creation, and achievement.

His multidisciplinary method bridges the gap between leading-edge technology, proven science, and ancient awareness-focusing practices, with a fresh, systematic, nonideological approach to mindfulness as its core. Together, these tools unlock the ability to create on an entirely different level and transform the journey from what is so often a tortuous experience into a revelatory quest to be embraced and enjoyed.

When not busy creating everything from books to businesses and blogs to paintings, you can usually find him dancing around his living room with his wife and daughter . . . or writing in the third person.

Connect with Jonathan:

www.JonathanFields.com
twitter.com/jonathanfields
linkedin.com/in/jonathanfields1
facebook.com/jonathanfields